Lonely planet Kids

THE DINOSAUR BOOK

THE DINOSAUR BOOK

Project managed by: Dynamo Limited
Author: Anne Rooney
Consultant: Dr David Button
Publisher: Piers Pickard
Editorial Director: Joe Fullman
Art Director: Andy Mansfield
Design and illustrations: Dynamo Limited
Print Production: Nigel Longuet

Published in October 2021 by Lonely Planet
Global Ltd
CRN: 554153
ISBN 978 1 83869 465 4

Printed in Singapore
10 9 8 7 6 5 4 3 2 1

STAY IN TOUCH:
lonelyplanet.com/contact

Lonely Planet Office:
IRELAND
Digital Depot, Roe Lane (off Thomas St), Digital
Hub, Dublin 8, D08 TCV4

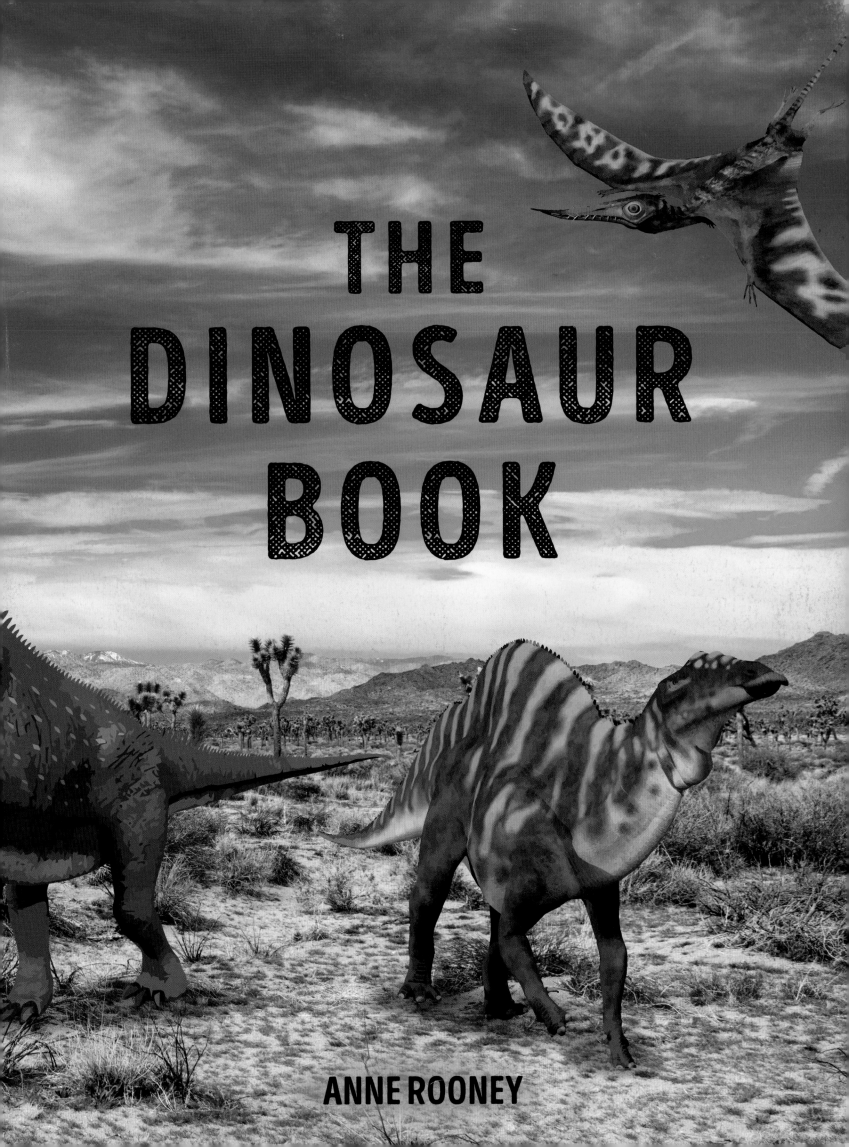

THE DINOSAUR BOOK

ANNE ROONEY

CONTENTS

DINOSAUR WORLD

Dinosaurs dominated our planet for more than 160 million years. They evolved and changed to adopt many different lifestyles and live in every type of environment. Some ate plants, others ate meat, fish, or eggs. Some lived in forests, others in deserts or plains. Some were huge, others small. Some hunted using vicious claws and teeth, while others defended themselves with spikes, horns and armor plates The dinosaurs were not alone—they shared the world with other reptiles that flew in the sky or swam in the seas. But it was dinosaurs that dominated in an age of reptiles that spanned nearly half the time animals have lived on land.

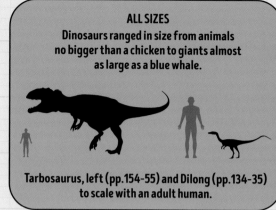

ALL SIZES
Dinosaurs ranged in size from animals no bigger than a chicken to giants almost as large as a blue whale.

Tarbosaurus, left (pp.154-55) and Dilong (pp.134-35) to scale with an adult human.

SHIFTING LANDS

The land in the time of the dinosaurs was not arranged as it is now. When dinosaurs first evolved, about 230 million years ago, almost all the land on Earth was connected in a single, large continent named Pangaea. Most of it was hot and dry, and not an easy place for animals to live. But Pangaea soon split apart. Over millions of years, seas divided the vast landmass into fragments. The changes affected the climate, making inland areas wetter. Huge forests began to grow, providing more places for animals to live. With Pangaea broken up, animals, including dinosaurs, that had once been able to roam freely over the entire Earth, became trapped in lands surrounded by sea.

In the early days of the dinosaurs, around 200 million years ago, most of the land was joined together, and blocks were just beginning to separate.

At the end of the dinosaurs' reign, 65.5 million years ago, the present continents were forming.

DIFFERING DINOS

The stranded groups of dinosaurs evolved separately, each adapting to conditions in the land where they lived. Although basic dinosaur bodies and shapes were the same around the world, they became different in their details. It's easy to see how animals such as stegosaurs all came from a single type of ancestor, but then grew apart over millions of years.

Stegosaurus (pp.48-49) lived in North America more than 5 million years after Huayangosaurus died out. Although similar to Huayangosaurus, it was much bigger, had large, broad plates on its back, and no shoulder spikes.

Huayangosaurus (pp.138-39) was a stegosaur from China. It had huge shoulder spikes that helped it to defend itself, two rows of narrow, spiky plates along its back, and a set of sharp spikes at the end of its tail.

DINOSAUR TIMELINE

Scientists divide prehistoric time into different periods. The dinosaurs lived in three periods: the Triassic (252–201 million years ago); the Jurassic (201–145 million years ago); and the Cretaceous (145–65.5 million years ago). Together, these periods are known as the Mesozoic Era.

MESOZOIC ERA

252
million years ago

201
million years ago

201
million years ago

145
million years ago

145
million years ago

65.5
million years ago

TRIASSIC

The Triassic came straight after a catastrophe, a mass extinction event, that killed more than 90 percent of all species living on Earth. It took a long time for life to recover. The first small, fast-running dinosaurs were among the new animals to evolve. Fossils of these Triassic dinosaurs are most often found in South America.

Herrerasaurus (pp.64-65), an early dinosaur from South America, lived before the dinosaurs split into groups with different body shapes..

JURASSIC

The Jurassic was the time of the giants, like Diplodocus (pp.24–25) and Brontosaurus. Other famous dinosaurs of this time include Stegosaurus (pp.40–41) and Allosaurus (pp.16–17).

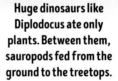

Huge dinosaurs like Diplodocus ate only plants. Between them, sauropods fed from the ground to the treetops.

CRETACEOUS

The Cretaceous saw some of the best-known dinosaurs, such as T. rex (pp.46–47), Triceratops (pp.43), Parasaurolophus (pp.32–33), and Ankylosaurus (pp.18–19). It also saw the end of the dinosaurs.

Dinosaurs such as Ankylosaurus had armor and spikes to protect themselves from large meat eaters like T. rex.

DINOSAUR DESIGNS

Experts divide dinosaurs into groups by their body types and behavior. As reptiles, all dinosaurs had four limbs, a tail, and a head and they laid eggs. There were two main groups: those with hips like those of modern lizards and those with hips more like modern birds (see p.110). But there was a lot of variation within these similarities. The birds around us today are the only surviving dinosaurs and, oddly, evolved from the lizard-hipped dinos.

ALL SHAPES AND SIZES

Dinosaurs are further divided into three main groups: theropods, sauropods, and ornithischians. All but the very earliest dinosaurs fall into one of these groups. The earliest dinosaurs often had features of more than one group and are hard to classify.

Dinosaurs like Saltasaurus (pp.68-69) are called sauropods. They walked on four legs, had long necks and tails, and ate plants. Most were so large that they were not in danger from meat-eating dinosaurs. Sauropods were lizard-hipped dinosaurs.

Theropods, like T. rex (pp.46-47), walked on two strong back legs and ate meat. They could generally run fast and had powerful jaws. Many of these had feathers, at least when they were young. Birds evolved from a group of theropods called dromeosaurs.

A final large group is the ornithischian dinosaurs. They had very varied body shapes, from stocky, slow animals like Ankylosaurus (pp.18-19) and Triceratops (pp.43), to more nimble animals that could run on two legs, like Parasaurolophus (pp.32-33). They were bird-hipped dinosaurs. All of these dinosaurs ate plants.

DINOSAUR LIVES

Like all animals, dinosaurs had to find food, find a mate, and have babies. Almost all lived on land, but a few types might have hunted for fish in rivers, and it's possible that Spinosaurus (pp.122–123) even swam in the sea. All types laid eggs, just as modern reptiles such as crocodiles and lizards do. Many probably laid a lot of eggs, as there were many dangers for a young dinosaur to face and few lived to be fully grown-up. They could be eaten by predators, suffer accidents and illnesses, or starve from lack of food.

Although Maiasaura (pp.30-31) grew to 29 ft. (9 m) long, the babies were only 12 in. (30 cm) long.

Pterosaurs ranged in size from a large bird to a small plane. Some hunted from the air, swooping over the sea to snatch fish, Others, like Thalassodromeus (pp.70-71), hunted on land.

DINOSAURS AND FRIENDS

Dinosaurs didn't have the planet to themselves. The seas were filled with fish, including sharks, and many types of invertebrates (animals without a backbone), such as jellyfish, sponges, ammonites, and squid. There were also giant marine reptiles, including pliosaurs, plesiosaurs, fish-shaped ichthyosaurs, and crocodile-like mosasaurs. On the land and in the skies, flying reptiles called pterosaurs swept around and above the dinosaurs. There were also other reptiles, including lizards, early birds (starting about 125 million years ago), many insects, and the first small mammals. Many marine and flying reptiles are also featured in this book alongside the dinosaurs.

Marine reptiles, like the pliosaur Kronosaurus (pp.172-73), lived in water and breathed air. They were all meat eaters, and some grew to enormous sizes.

Some mammals, like Xianshou, lived 160 million years ago in the trees of China. Others burrowed underground or found different ways to avoid the heavy feet and sharp teeth of dinosaurs.

DINOSAURS AND ENEMIES

Although some dinosaurs were the largest animals living in their time and place, they were far from indestructible. Large dinosaurs ate small dinosaurs. They fought over food, mates, land to live in, and perhaps over which dinosaur should be in charge of a herd. They had accidents, caught illnesses, and were plagued by biting bugs and other parasites.

This sauropod had a disease in its bones that caused pain and skin ulcers.

BACK FROM THE DEAD!

If you had lived 200 years ago, you would have known nothing about dinosaurs, not even that they had existed. That might seem strange, since dinosaurs lived millions of years ago. But we've only known about them since their fossilized remains have been collected and examined.

UNEARTHED

The first bit of dinosaur bone was found in 1646 in England, although no one at the time knew what it was. Only a sketch and a description survive. More fossils were found in the 1800s. In 1842, the English biologist Richard Owen realized there were similarities between the bones being found and that they all belonged to large, extinct reptiles. He used the word "dinosaur," which means "terrible lizard," to describe them. At the time, only three dinosaurs were known: Megalosaurus (pp.90–91), Iguanodon (pp.86–87), and Hylaeosaurus.

The chunk of bone discovered in 1646 was probably part of the thigh bone of a Megalosaurus

FOSSIL HUNTING

Today, fossil hunting is very different to those early years. Experts, called paleontologists, know where to look for fossils and which types of rocks are likely to contain them. When a fossil is discovered, its exact position is recorded and the parts are removed slowly and carefully. The arrangement of the parts is recorded with photographs and sketches, and even the tiniest pieces are removed carefully. Paleontologists use tools ranging from diggers and shovels to small probes and brushes. They figure out the age of fossils from the rocks they are found in by using radioactive dating. This uses the way chemicals change over millions of years to show experts how long a fossil has been buried.

Separating fossils from the rocks they are found in is a painstaking process that can take months or years.

FROM BONE TO STONE

Most fossils are of the hard parts of animals, such as bones, teeth, horns, and claws. These "body fossils" can form if a dead animal is quickly covered with water and sediment, such as mud or sand, before scavengers have eaten or destroyed it. Over a very long time, chemical changes take place in the hard body parts, turning them to stone. The sediment is squashed and turns to rock, too. The result is a body fossil encased in rock. Often, these remain buried far underground, but occasionally changes in the landscape mean they are brought to the surface and we can find them.

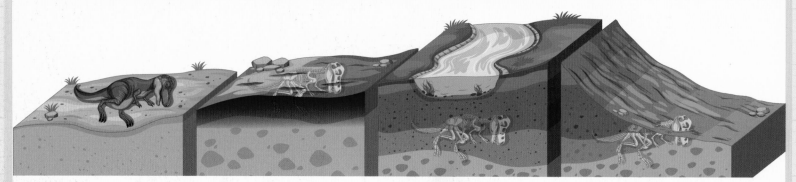

An animal dies.

The body is covered with water and mud or sand.

This is squashed and turns to rock. More sediment creates layers on top of layers.

Landslips, battering by stormy seas, or quarrying can all reveal hidden fossils.

LESSONS FROM FOSSILS

Scientists can learn a lot from fossils of dinosaurs. The shape and size of bones can reveal information such as how fast they could walk or run, and whether they went on two feet or four. The shape of the teeth can tell us whether they ate meat or plants. Skin impressions show whether they were feathery or scaly or had bony plates, and so on. Just sometimes, fossil hunters find other traces of animals, such as footprints, the marks made by tails, eggshells, and even fossilized poop!

TEETH

Teeth tell us what dinosaurs ate. Long sharp teeth with a sawlike edge show the dinosaur ate meat. Many small teeth with a straight edge, or a mouth with a sharp beak, show the dinosaur fed on plants.

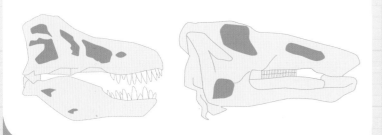

The shape of the teeth show that the skull on the left is a carnivore's and the one on the right belongs to a herbivore.

KNOWING AND NOT KNOWING

It's harder to find out some other details of dinosaur lives and bodies. We can rarely tell what kind of noise they made, or what color they were, what their nests were like, or whether they looked after their young. We often don't even have a full skeleton to work from. Very, very few of the dinosaurs that ever lived have been fossilized and many must still lie buried and undiscovered. The pictures in this book don't show you exactly what dinosaurs looked like, but the experts' best current guess. The dinosaurs in the book might be dead, but dinosaur studies are very much alive, and dinosaurs are changing all the time!

TOP TRACKS

Footprints can be preserved if they quickly fill with sediment and then dry out and bake hard. From footprints, experts can figure out how heavy an animal was, how it moved, and how fast it could go. It's not always easy to tell exactly which animal made the tracks, though.

Huge theropod footprints like these were first found in 1802. At the time, people guessed they were created by giant birds!

POOP PROOF

Coprolites are fossilized poop or stomach contents. Even though the food has been broken down, scientists can tell what kind of food the animal ate from fragments of bone, seed, feathers, and other evidence.

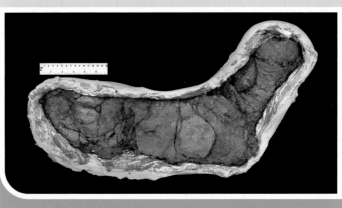

This coprolite comes from a meat-eating dinosaur.

END OF THE DINOSAURS

All the non-bird dinosaurs suddenly disappeared from the fossil record over a short time 65.5 million years ago. The last of the large marine reptiles and the pterosaurs disappeared at the same time. Most experts agree that they were all wiped out when a massive asteroid crashed into Earth. The impact would have hurled rock dust and ash into the air, shrouding Earth with thick clouds that would have made it cold for years. Blocking the sunlight would have killed plants and then the animals that relied on them would have died, too. When Earth finally settled, new types of life arose to dominate—the mammals that had been small during the age of dinosaurs took over.

A massive rock from space crashing into Earth caused immediate devastation and changed the climate for years.

NORTH AMERICA

North America is very rich in dinosaur fossils, including many of the most popular and famous, from the Jurassic Diplodocus (pp.24-25) and Stegosaurus (pp.40-41) to the late Cretaceous T. rex (pp.46-47) and Triceratops (pp.43). While these giants lumbered across the land, huge plesiosaurs swam in the surrounding sea, and pterosaurs soared above them.

DEINONYCHUS (pp.22-23)
Wyoming, USA

MAIASAURA (pp.30-31)
Montana, USA

TYRANNOSAURUS REX (pp.46-47)
Alberta, Canada

TRICERATOPS (p.43)
Alberta, Canada

STEGOCERAS (pp.38-39)
Montana to New Mexico, USA

ELASMOSAURUS (pp.26-27)
Western Interior Seaway

QUETZALCOATLUS (pp.36-37)
Texas, USA

UTAHRAPTOR (pp.48-49)
Utah, USA

CHICXULUB CRATER (pp.50-51)
Mexico

ALBERTOSAURUS (p14-15)
Mexico and Canada

SEA SPLIT

North America looked very different 90 million years ago. A sea, called the Western Interior Seaway, split the continent from north to south, and was bordered by forests of conifers, cycads, and tree ferns. Between the forests and rivers stretched vast plains of ferns—there were no grasses yet. The west of North America was the stomping ground of some of the most famous dinosaurs of all time.

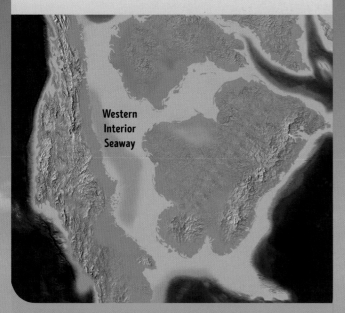

Western Interior Seaway

In the Cretaceous, North America was split into three main blocks of land.

The first dinosaur fossils found in North America were the footprints of a giant theropod, but scientists at the time believed them to have been made by a giant bird. Confusingly, huge meat-eating "terror" birds did live in North America—but not until long after the dinosaurs died out.

FIRST FINDS

In 1838, a man in New Jersey called John Estaugh Hopkins found large bones in a pit, which he stored in his house. Twenty years later, the rest of the skeleton was dug up and examined by an expert, Joseph Leidy, who named it Hadrosaurus. It was the first American dinosaur, but would soon be followed by many more.

In 1868, Hadrosaurus became the first dinosaur skeleton mounted for public display, though in a pose we now know to be wrong.

BONE WARS

The dry, exposed, rocky "Badlands" of the Western USA (shown here) provided rich pickings as fossils became big business in the 19th century. Two competing fossil hunters dominated the search, Othniel Marsh and Edward Drinker Cope. Their methods were often underhanded and they even destroyed some fossils as they tried to beat each other to the best finds. Between them, March and Cope found some of the world's most famous dinosaurs, including Diplodocus (pp.24–25) and Triceratops (pp.43).

In the end, Marsh (left) found 80 new dinosaurs and Cope 56.

ALBERTOSAURUS

The first dinosaur discovered in Canada was Albertosaurus, a fierce animal that terrorized the lush forests of Cretaceous Alberta. It probably hunted in packs—large numbers have been found buried together. A pack of Albertosaurus would have been a terrifying sight for any prey animal.

NORTH AMERICA

FACT FILE

Name: *Albertosaurus sarcophagus*
Lived: Alberta (Canada), Mexico; 70-68 million years ago
Size: Weight 5,800 lb. (2,600 kg); length 29 ft. (9 m)
Diet: Meat, including other dinosaurs
Discovered: In 1884 by Joseph B Tyrrell; named in 1905 by Henry Fairfield Osborn

To scale with adult human

FLESH EATER

Albertosaurus's full name is *Albertosaurus sarcophagus*. The second part means "flesh eater," and it certainly lived up to its name. Its huge, banana-shaped fangs could grasp a struggling animal without being yanked from its jaw by another dino. It could have eaten any of the large plant-eating dinosaurs of North America, probably preferring hadrosaurs. Albertosaurus was much lighter than the herbivores and might have preferred to pick off young, smaller, or sick animals if it was hunting alone.

Small ornithopods would have been an easy meal for Albertosaurus.

Albertosaurus had huge, muscular rear legs that helped it to run fast.

Eye socket

Nostril

BIG EYES

Large holes in the skull helped to keep Albertosaurus's head light. The eye sat in the middle of the three large holes The small holes at the front of the skull were its nostrils.

The three large openings in Albertosaurus's skull are separated by thin struts of bone.

Short bony lumps above the eyes might have been brightly colored. They could have been used to attract a mate or just to help Albertosaurus spot others of the same species.

Some of the teeth have a jagged edge like a saw. That would have helped Albertosaurus to rip through flesh by gripping tightly and pulling its head back.

The skull was nearly 3 ft. (1 m) long and was packed with more than 60 teeth.

A FIGHTING CHANCE

Having many fossils of an animal helps scientists figure out their life history. A few fossils of young Albertosaurus, aged 2 to 11, have been found at Horseshoe Canyon in Canada. The fossils suggest that a hatchling that made it to the age of two stood a good chance of survival until the start of its teenage growth spurt at the age of 12. A two-year-old Albertosaurus would have been larger than any other predator in its area except an adult Albertosaurus.

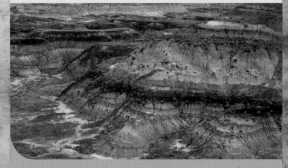

Many dinosaur fossils, including Albertosaurus, are found in the exposed rock layers of Horseshoe Canyon in Canada.

Experts don't know what Albertosaurus used its hands for. Its arms were too short to hold food near its mouth or to help it get up from the ground.

SCARY KIDS

An Albertosaurus fossilized at around two years old shows the babies grew quickly. It was already 6 ft. (2 m) long and would have weighed 110 lb. (50 kg)—as much as a small adult human. The youngsters could probably run more quickly than the adults and might have chased prey animals toward waiting adults for them to kill.

ALLOSAURUS

Allosaurus was the earliest and first truly big and scary theropod found. It lived long before the more famous T. rex and was discovered before it, too. It was a very common dinosaur in Jurassic North America. It lived in areas of flat floodplains where there were clear wet and dry seasons during the year.

NORTH AMERICA

FACT FILE

Name: *Allosaurus fragilis*
Lived: Wyoming, Colorado, Utah (USA); also Portugal, Siberia, Tanzania; 155-150 million years ago
Size: Weight 5,500 lb. (2,500 kg); length 29 ft. (9 m)
Diet: Plant-eating dinosaurs
Discovered: In 1869 by Ferdinand Hayden; named in 1877 by Othniel Marsh

To scale with adult human

FAST FOOD

Allosaurus was a meat eater but it's not quite clear exactly what it ate. It could have eaten medium-sized ornithopods but they could run quite quickly. Even though Allosaurus could probably reach a top speed of 21 mph (34 km/h), catching a speedy ornithopod might have been tricky.

Eating large animals was hard on Allosaurus's teeth. They often came out in its food, but were quickly replaced by new ones.

Small horn-like bumps above its eyes, and ridges of bone running from them to the end of the nose, made Allosaurus's face different from other theropods.

DANGEROUS DINNER

Perhaps Allosaurus hunted much slower animals, like Stegosaurus, but they were spiky and quite dangerous to grapple with. Allosaurus have been found with evidence of injuries inflicted by Stegosaurus, as well as Stegosaurus found with bite marks from an Allosaurus.

An adult Stegosaurus (right) might well have had to protect its young from an attack by an Allosaurus.

BIG AL'S AILMENTS

One of the most complete Allosaurus skeletons ever found has been named "Big Al," although he wasn't fully grown when he died. Found in 1991 in Wyoming, USA, Big Al had a lot wrong with him. His bones show he had several injuries and infections, especially in his feet and legs. In some places, extra bone had grown to cover damage. Hunting would have been difficult and painful, so he may have died of hunger.

IDENTITY CRISIS

Local people thought the very first Allosaurus bones found were horses' hooves that had been petrified (turned to stone). They were wrongly identified as a form of the European dinosaur Poekilopleuron and then named Antrodemus. Allosaurus has been "found" and named many times since. Further Allosaurus remains were named Creosaurus, Labrosaurus, and Epanterias.

SAUROPOD SNACK

Allosaurus might have tackled sauropods. In the areas of North America where it lived, there was plenty of variety, including Diplodocus, Camarasaurus, and Brontosaurus. But these animals were much bigger than Allosaurus. Unless it hunted in packs, Allosaurus would do best to pick off weak or young individuals. Or it could just bite large chunks out of a fleeing sauropod that it could easily outrun.

Its large jaws and wide gape would have been suited to biting chunks out of its prey, which would soon die of blood loss.

Fragments of one individual Allosaurus show it may have been much larger than all the others—about a fifth larger at nearly 39 ft. (12 m) long.

A quarry in Utah, USA, contains the greatest number of Jurassic dinosaur fossils in the world. Of the 46 dinosaurs in it, 74 are Allosaurus.

An individual Allosaurus was probably fully grown at the age of 15 but didn't live beyond about 30 years old.

COLLECTED DINO

One of the most complete Allosaurus skeletons ever found lay unexamined in a crate of fossils for many years. Owned by paleontologist Edward Cope, the crate was not opened until six years after his death. Cope and his rival Othniel Marsh were often so busy collecting bones, trying to find more fossils than each other, that they had little time left to examine them.

Cope's Allosaurus was one of the first dinosaurs mounted in a realistic pose.

ANKYLOSAURUS

Built like an armored tank and with a bony tail club, Ankylosaurus was well protected against most enemies. For its survival, this plant eater relied on making itself almost impossible to eat by predators that roamed the same region, including its main threat, the terrifying T. rex.

NORTH AMERICA

FACT FILE
Name: *Ankylosaurus magniventris*
Lived: Alberta (Canada), Montana, Wyoming (USA); 68-66 million years ago
Size: Weight 11,000 lb. (5,000 kg); length up to 33 ft. (10 m)
Diet: Low-growing plants
Discovered: In 1906 by Peter Kaisen; named in 1908 by Barnum Brown

To scale with adult human

EXTREME SURVIVAL
To defend itself, Ankylosaurus evolved a hard outside armor. All of its exposed surfaces were covered with bony plates, called osteoderms, which were difficult for teeth or claws to penetrate. These grew within the skin, like the scales of a crocodile, and were also covered with a layer of keratin—the same material that your hair and nails are made of!

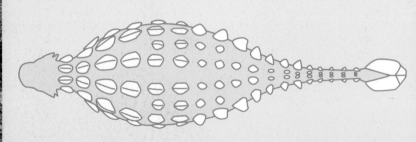

The best-protected area was the neck, where a predator's bite would have caused most harm.

As well as armor, Ankylosaurus had spikes around its head and tail, and conical horns in rows along its back and sides.

The tail club could grow to at least 24 in. (60 cm) long and 19 in. (49 cm) wide.

Ankylosaurus tail club, top view

This is the only surviving fossil of an ankylosaurus tail club.

A TAIL LIKE A HAMMER
At the end of its tail, Ankylosaurus had a large, bony club that it could swing from side to side, smashing the leg bones of anything trying to attack it. Some of its vertebrae were fused together, making the tail like a rod, so it was stronger and more effective as a club.

NOT QUITE RIGHT...

Ankylosaurus was first found without its tail club and with other parts missing. It was recreated copying some features from Stegosaurus, which was a very different shape. That created an animal with a high, domed back, long rear legs, and a tail just reaching to the ground. In fact, Ankylosaurus was very low and flat, with front and rear legs about the same length.

BITING WITH A BEAK

Ankylosaurus grazed on low-growing plants, such as ferns and shrubs, which it stripped and snipped with a beak-like mouth. Breaking down its food happened mainly in its large gut. Like many plant-eaters, it probably had microbes in its gut, which helped to break down its food.

Like Ankylosaurus, a modern tortoise has a hard, strong beak.

Its eyelids were protected with armor and by bony points above the eyes.

On its short legs, Ankylosaurus couldn't move quickly. Its top speed was probably 6 mph (10 km/h).

It was so wide and low to the ground that it would have been difficult for a predator to get hold of Ankylosaurus or turn it over to attack its soft belly.

CAMARASAURUS

Camarasaurus tramped through the Jurassic forests, perhaps in family groups or herds. A lot of Camarasaurus fossils survive, so these sauropods were probably a common sight in their day. As long as a large helicopter, the dinosaur was still only medium-sized for a sauropod.

NORTH AMERICA

FACT FILE
Name: *Camarasaurus supremus*
Lived: Colorado, Wyoming, Utah, New Mexico (USA); 150-145 million years ago
Size: Weight 44,000 lb. (20,000 kg); length 49-75 ft. (15-23 m)
Diet: Tough vegetation
Discovered: In 1877 by Oramel W. Lucas; named in 1877 by Edward Drinker Cope

To scale with adult human

AIRY BONES

Camarasaurus means "chambered lizard," which is a reference to the holes inside its vertebrae. These hollows indicate the presence of a system of air sacs—like those of modern birds—that would have helped the dinosaur to breathe. It was a long way down a sauropod's neck: the air sacs in the body would have acted like bellows, drawing air down the long, narrow neck, then driving it first through the lungs, and then up through the neck, and out through the mouth and nose again.

Camarasaurus had light bones because of the air sacs.

Camarasaurus may have had a row of short spikes along its back, called neural spines.

MISSING TOES

Camarasaurus had three claws on each back foot. But it probably had just a single toe on each front foot. The bones for other toes were there but hidden within the foot. Only one toe—or maybe a claw— was on the outside.

Camarasaurus may have used the claws on its back feet for digging soil.

HEAD HELD HIGH

Unlike many other sauropods, Camarasaurus could hold its neck upright and browse on leaves high in the trees. Most other sauropods that lived at the same time fed at lower levels. Even so, its neck was not especially long for its body length, making Camarasaurus short and stocky for a sauropod.

Chomping through tons of tough leaves wears out the teeth. Camarasaurus replaced its teeth every 62 days.

BUYING BONES

Edward Drinker Cope bought several wagon-loads of assorted dinosaur bones from fossil hunter Oramel Lucas, who had a fossil quarry in Colorado. Bones of the Camarasaurus were in one of the loads.

Camarasaurus eggs were buried in a row rather than in a nest. This suggests Camarasaurus parents paid little attention to them.

LEAVING SOME LEAVES FOR OTHERS

Camarasaurus lived alongside several different types of sauropods. All sauropods ate plants, and each one needed to eat a lot. To prevent species fighting for food, each specialized in different foods. We can tell what each type of sauropod ate from the shape of the teeth. The Camarasaurus had teeth with sharp edges, ideal for snipping off leaves and slicing them up.

Camarasaurus's teeth were deeply rooted in thick gums, so they looked much shorter in life than in its skeleton.

DEINONYCHUS

About the weight of a large wolf, Deinonychus was a theropod that scampered through the warm woodlands of the western USA, feasting on the small local plant eaters. Though it looks similar to many other small theropods, Deinonychus has had a big impact on how we now think about dinosaurs.

NORTH AMERICA

FACT FILE
Name: *Deinonychus antirrhopus*
Lived: Utah, Wyoming, Montana, Oklahoma (USA); 120-110 million years ago
Size: Weight 165 lb. (75 kg); length 13 ft. (4 m)
Diet: Plant-eating dinosaurs, small animals
Discovered: In 1903 by Barnum Brown; named in 1969 by John Ostrom

To scale with adult human

The shape of Deinonychus's skull tells us a lot about its brain. Large regions for sight and smell show it could see very well and had a good sense of smell —useful for a predator.

SPARKING A REVOLUTION

The description of Deinonychus in 1969 sparked a re-think of dinosaur science. Before then, people thought dinosaurs were huge, lumbering, sluggish, cold-blooded beasts, like giant lizards, that needed sun to help them move quickly. Deinonychus didn't look as if it was ever sluggish. It was slender, with long legs and light bones, which meant it could run fast.

A modern lizard is cold-blooded and can run fast only when warmed by the sun.

GETTING IN A FLAP

Its front limbs were probably feathered, though it's unlikely Deinonychus could fly. Flapping its feathered arms would have helped it to keep its balance while holding down a wriggling meal— just as you might flail your arms if you feel you're falling. However, there is no fossil evidence that Deinonychus had feathers.

BALANCING TAIL

Deinonychus's whole body was well suited to clinging to prey and tearing pieces off. It had a stiff tail that worked as a counterbalance to the heavy head to stop it falling over. This worked a little like a seesaw: when the head went up, the tail would go down, and when the head went down, the tail would go up.

Deinonychus could have been a very fast animal, or it might have been built for strength and only fairly fast. Its long shin bones suggest speed, but as some relatives of Deinonychus were not very fast, either is possible.

TERRIBLE CLAW

The most striking feature of Deinonychus is an extra-large claw on the second toe of each hind foot. The claw could grow to 5 in. (12 cm) long— enough to rip into or pin down a smaller animal. It's likely that Deinonychus used it to hold down a struggling animal while biting into it, as some modern-day birds of prey do.

Terrible claw

Deinonychus means "terrible claw" and its claws would have inflicted some serious injuries.

The very long tail was stiffened and kept very straight, with just a little side-to-side movement.

TREE HUGGER

Deinonychus could possibly climb trees, using its claws to hold onto the bark. Their hooked shape could have supported the lightweight animal, just as the claws of a domestic cat help it to climb a tree.

UNSOLVED MYSTERY

Deinonychus's shape suggests that perhaps some dinosaurs were warm-blooded. This means they could move equally quickly in warm or cold weather, by day or by night. The question still being asked is: Were all dinosaurs warm-blooded? If so, at which stage of their history did they become warm-blooded? The experts still don't know.

When Deinonychus wasn't using its rear claws, it held them up off the ground, to keep them sharp and undamaged.

Being small and light might have helped with tree climbing.

DIPLODOCUS

Diplodocus was a plant-eating sauropod of unimaginable size. It's one of the longest dinosaurs known from a complete skeleton. It was certainly large enough to have no natural enemies once it was fully grown, being too big for any predator to tackle.

NORTH AMERICA

To scale with adult human

IN AND OUT OF THE FOREST

Diplodocus was far too big to push its way through a dense forest. Adult Diplodocus probably lived on the plains, in sparsely wooded areas, and at the edges of denser woodland. There, they could both feed on low-growing plants and eat from trees. Baby Diplodocus, though, would have been in danger from predators, particularly on open ground. The young might have run into the undergrowth of the forest when they hatched. Large predators would have the same problem fitting between the trees as adult sauropods.

Most of a Diplodocus was neck and tail. Its neck was 26 ft. (8 m) long and its tail 46 ft. (14 m) long.

CAST IN PLASTER

Many museums around the world have plaster casts of the same Diplodocus fossil, found in 1898 and known as Dippy. Casts are a way of exhibiting accurate copies of fossils so that people around the world can enjoy them.

Plaster casts of Dippy first went on display in 1905.

DIPPY DIDN'T DROOP

Early drawings often showed Diplodocus with its tail drooping and dragging on the ground and its neck lowered. Diplodocus could lift its head to eat from trees, and could even rear up on its hind legs. Usually, though, it held its neck and tail out fairly straight, sweeping its head from side to side to eat low-growing plants around it.

Early experts thought Dippy's tail drooped (above) but tendons attached to bones in the tail held the tail up effortlessly.

Diplodocus possibly grew to its adult size in only 10 years—starting from an egg that weighed just 3 lb. (1.5 kg) and was about the size of a soccer ball.

Diplodocus could crack its tail like a whip, swishing it so fast that the end broke the sound barrier and made a noise like a canon firing.

LEGS LIKE COLUMNS

In the early 1900s, people thought sauropods were so heavy they must have lived in the water, with the water supporting their weight. They didn't, but you still sometimes see pictures of sauropods lounging in lakes. Instead, their thick legs and column-like feet supported their weight on land.

ELASMOSAURUS

A sea creature that was mostly neck, Elasmosaurus swam in the Western Interior Seaway near the end of the age of the dinosaurs. It was one of the largest of the plesiosaurs, a type of marine reptile. These reptiles had returned to the sea from being land animals, their four limbs evolving into flippers.

NORTH AMERICA

FACT FILE
Name: *Elasmosaurus platyurus*
Lived: Western Interior Seaway; 94–71 million years ago
Size: Length 33 ft. (10 m); neck 23 ft. (7 m)
Diet: Fish
Discovered: In 1868 by Theophilus Turner; named in 1869 by Edward Drinker Cope

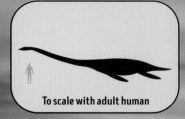

To scale with adult human

FLAPPING FLIPPERS

Although they were great for moving through water, its flippers would have made it impossible for Elasmosaurus to move on land. Getting ashore to lay eggs would have been virtually impossible, so Elasmosaurus probably gave birth to live babies in the sea. Even if it could have dragged itself along with its flippers, its huge weight would have made movement on land and breathing in air difficult.

Elasmosaurus needed the water to support its weight.

SNAPPY!

Elasmosaurus fed on fish. A shoal of fish swimming above it would have cast a shadow against the bright surface of the water. With its very long neck, Elasmosaurus could snap up individuals without needing to swim after them—an advantage for a large and possibly slow-swimming animal.

Elasmosaurus probably hunted fish from below, catching them with its sharp teeth.

Its flippers were quite stiff, and Elasmosaurus used them like paddles to propel itself and to steer.

COMING UP FOR AIR

Like modern marine mammals, such as seals, whales, and dolphins, Elasmosaurus would have come to the surface to breathe air, perhaps every 10 or 20 minutes. Although early pictures often show it holding its neck upright out of the water, Elasmosaurus didn't have the muscles to do that. It probably just popped its head above the surface to breathe before submerging again. Its babies would have had to come to the surface soon after birth to take a first breath.

Marine mammals, such as this humpback whale, have to surface to breathe air.

The needle-sharp narrow teeth stuck forward from the front of the jaw.

The second part of the name, platyurus, means "flat-tailed"—but in fact the flattened bones are in the neck.

TEETH LIKE A TRAP

Like many other fish-eating animals, Elasmosaurus had teeth that were ideal for piercing and trapping slippery fish. When the mouth closed, the interlocking teeth made an inescapable trap for the fish, which were then swallowed whole—the animal had no chewing teeth.

A TAIL ON THE FRONT?

The 19th-century fossil hunter Edward Drinker Cope thought the very long neck of the Elasmosaurus was a very long tail. When his mistake was pointed out, Cope tried to destroy all copies of his paper on Elasmosaurus. But his rival, Othniel Charles Marsh, saw the original and was quick to gloat over the mistake, making relations between the rivals even worse.

The first picture of Elasmosaurus (top), drawn from its fossil remains, put the head on the wrong end!

HESPERORNIS

Birds evolved from theropod dinosaurs in the Jurassic, but by the late Cretaceous, a few had given up some bird behaviors, such as flying. Hesperornis was a giant flightless bird. It lived in the sea, where it swam like a penguin and probably spent time on rocks to escape seagoing predators.

NORTH AMERICA

FACT FILE

Name: *Hesperornis regalis*
Lived: Canada, Kansas (USA), Russia, Sweden; 83.5–78 million years ago
Size: Length 6 ft. (1.8 m)
Diet: Fish
Discovered: In 1871 by Othniel Marsh; named in 1872 by Othniel Marsh

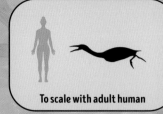

To scale with adult human

FLIGHTLESS AND WINGLESS

Wings first evolved in flying animals, but they have been used in other ways since. Large flightless birds, such as ostriches, use their wings in mating displays and fights, and for balance while running. Penguin wings have evolved into flippers. Hesperornis's wings were reduced to small stumps. It had no hand or lower arm bones, and the wing stopped at the elbow. This gave its body a streamlined shape helpful for swimming.

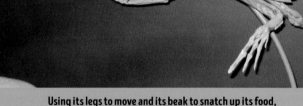

Using its legs to move and its beak to snatch up its food, Hesperornis had no need for front limbs.

Although many fossils of Hesperornis survive, we have only one nearly complete head, so there is more to learn about its jaw and teeth.

LOCKING TEETH

Hesperornis had teeth in the back part of its upper jaw and along most of its lower jaw, with just the tip left toothless. The teeth sat in a long continuous groove along the jaw bones, rather than each tooth having its own hole, or socket (as your teeth do). The teeth were unusual in another way, too. Small pits in the upper jaw lined up with the lower teeth, acting as sockets to hold the tips of the teeth when Hesperornis closed its mouth.

The tip of of the jaw was covered in keratin, giving Hesperornis a beak.

EARLY BIRDS

Hesperornis, along with another early bird, Ichthyornis, helped to persuade early dinosaur scientists that birds and reptiles are closely related. Ichthyornis could fly, and had legs suited to walking on land, but had the same pattern of teeth and beak as Hesperornis.

Ichthyornis looked rather like a modern seabird.

The feathers of water-going birds are kept sleek and waterproof with oil from the animal's body. This might have been true of Hesperornis, too.

Unlike dinosaurs, Hesperornis had kneecaps. In fact, its kneecap was huge—a spike-shaped bone almost as long as its thigh bone.

HUGE FLIPPER-FEET

Hesperornis had very large feet. The legs were set a long way back, which would be good for swimming, but not for walking. The toes may have been webbed or joined by flaps of skin. Either would have helped push against water as Hesperornis swam, working like flippers. On land, the bird possibly shuffled along and could have been easily attacked by meat-eating dinosaurs and flying pterosaurs.

The sleek, streamlined body shape made moving through water easy. Seals and penguins have evolved to have a similar shape. Hesperornis was covered with feathers.

DANGEROUS SEAS

The Cretaceous sea was no place for a leisurely swim. Hesperornis hunted fish, but was hunted itself. It would have made a welcome meal for huge fish like the 20 ft. (6 m) long Xiphactinus, sharks, or mosasaurs such as Tylosaurus and Plesiosaurs.

This Tylosaurus was found with the remains of a Hesperornis in its stomach.

Hesperornis was probably more like a wingless cormorant than any other modern bird.

MAIASAURA

Maiasuaura were hadrosaurs, plant-eating dinosaurs with a beak-like mouth. The discovery in 1979 of a site containing Maiasaura nests, nicknamed "Egg Mountain," excited dinosaur scientists as it showed the first evidence of dinosaurs caring for their young.

NORTH AMERICA

FACT FILE

Name: *Maiasaura peeblesorum*
Lived: Montana (USA); 80-75 million years ago
Size: Weight 5,500 lb. (2,500 kg); length 30 ft. (9 m)
Diet: Wood, tree bark and leaves from plants such as cycads, horsetails, and conifers
Discovered: In 1978 by Marion Brandvold; named in 1979 by Jack Horner and Robert Makela

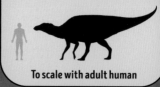
To scale with adult human

DINO NURSERY

Egg Mountain held the fossilized bones of around 200 Maiasaura, ranging in age from newly hatched infants to fully grown adults. Some of the fossilized bones were from new hatchlings, but others were from older infants, showing that the parents and young stayed together. The hatchlings had poorly developed rear legs, and so the parents must have brought food for them until they were old enough to forage for themselves, another sign of good parenting.

A hatchling grew from 19-118 in. (50-300 cm) long in just one year.

Adult Maiasaura usually walked on four legs, but could probably balance on two legs. Infants scurried around on just their hind legs, but switched to four legs as they grew.

WARM, LIKE COMPOST

A dinosaur that weighs thousands of pounds couldn't sit on her eggs—she'd be far too heavy. Instead, Maiasaura covered their eggs with a layer of vegetation. This would slowly break down in the hot, humid air, keeping the eggs warm while they incubated, just as a compost heap is warm on the inside.

Incubated egg hatching

The name Maiasaura means "good mother lizard," and unlike some dinosaurs, Maiasaura kept their young warm and safe.

A newly hatched Maiasaura was only 14 in. (35 cm) long, but by the age of seven or eight, it would have grown to adult size—25 times as long!

IN THE MIDDLE

Maiasaura lived in herds of up to hundreds of animals, which gave them protection. Predators might pick off weak animals at the edges of a herd, but the young could shelter in the middle. Wildebeest in Africa do this to protect their young from lions, hyenas, and leopards.

Wildebeest surround their young to protect them from predators.

Maiasaura had no defense against predators. Even their tails were too stiff to swing.

HIGH-RISK INFANCY

Only around one in ten baby Maiasaura survived their first year, and those that did had a good chance of growing up. But by the age of eight, life became risky again, with about a 45 percent chance of dying. However, growing quickly meant the young were most vulnerable for only a short period. Maiasaura could breed at an early age, so although many died, there were a lot around.

Like other hadrosaurs, Maiasaura had much shorter front legs than back legs.

Although this shows only a few, there were usually 35–40 eggs in a nest.

PARASAUROLOPHUS

A dinosaur with a huge head crest, Parasaurolophus lived in herds in the woodlands of the west. When it was first discovered, some scientists thought that the head crest could have been used as a snorkel or air tank, allowing the dinosaur to spend most of its time underwater!

NORTH AMERICA

FACT FILE
Name: *Parasaurolophus walkeri*
Lived: Alberta (Canada), Utah, New Mexico (USA); 76-74 million years ago
Size: Weight 7,700 lb. (3,500 kg); length 29 ft. (9 m)
Diet: Tough plants
Discovered: In 1920 by field workers from the University of Toronto; named by William A. Parks in 1922

To scale with adult human

BUILT-IN TRUMPET
Parasaurolophus is known for its head crest. The crest could have worked rather like a trumpet, amplifying sounds, so that the Parasaurolophus's honks and hoots would resound through the woodland. Larger adults made low sounds that would carry a long way, while the young made higher-pitched sounds. It makes sense for the infants' sounds to be heard nearby by a parent, rather than further off by a predator.

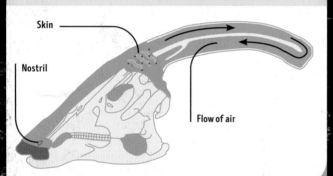

Skin

Nostril

Flow of air

Inside the crest, hollow tubes run from each nostril to the end of the crest and then back along the crest and into the lungs.

The skull, with its crest, grew to 5.2 ft. (1.6 m)—the size of a short adult human.

GROWING A CREST
Baby Parasaurolophus did not hatch with a head crest. A young animal, 6 ft. (2 m) long, has been found with a partly grown crest that is low and rounded. It would have become long and narrow later.

The crest on a young Parasaurolophus was like a small bump on the top of its head.

Parasaurolophus used four legs while walking and foraging for food, and two legs to hurry away from danger. The young trotted along on two legs.

KNOW ME, KNOW MY CREST

A brightly colored head crest could have been used for identification. A colorful crest might have attracted a mate, or marked the difference between males and females, or might just have been a way for individuals to recognize others from their species or herd. The crest might have been joined to the neck with a flap of skin, too, which would give extra space for showy colors.

The structure of Parasaurolophus's ears show they had good hearing.

The large head crest was an extension of the tip of its upper jaw and its nose bones.

DUCK-BILLED

Hadrosaurs like Parasaurolophus were duck-billed dinosaurs, which means they had a mouth a little like a duck's bill, wide and flat at the front. Although it had no teeth at the front, it had plenty further back. Parasaurolophus would snip through twigs with the bill and then chew its food further back, using rows of up to 300 teeth. These were closely packed rows of teeth that were replaced as they wore out, with new teeth moving forward from behind.

Teeth arranged in blocks of five or six gave Parasaurolophus a good, broad surface for grinding up tough plant matter.

Hadrosaurs like Parasaurolophus had extra flesh around their fingers, making their hands look rather like mittens.

PTERANODON

A flying reptile called a pterosaur, Pteranodon was not a dinosaur but flew in the skies above the dinosaurs of North America. Birds didn't descend from pterosaurs, though the earliest birds shared the sky with them. Pterosaurs were wiped out with the dinosaurs 65.5 million years ago.

NORTH AMERICA

FACT FILE

Name: *Pteranodon longiceps*
Lived: Alabama, Nebraska, Wyoming, South Dakota (USA); 85-75 million years ago
Size: Weight 20-29 lb. (9-13 kg); wingspan 10-20 ft. (3-6 m)
Diet: Fish, small animals
Discovered: In 1870 by Samuel Wendell Williston; named in 1876 by Othniel Marsh

To scale with adult human

ATTACHED WINGS

Unlike bird wings, Pteranodon's wings consisted of skin stretched between the front and rear limbs. The skin was attached near the ankle, or perhaps closer to the body—it's impossible to tell from fossils. The fourth finger was greatly extended, running from the joint to the tip of the wing, making the leading edge of the wing. The other fingers had shorter claws at the joint that would normally be the wrist.

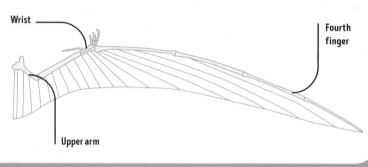

Wrist

Fourth finger

Upper arm

All pterosaur wings had a short upper arm and a very long fourth finger. They also had a bone found in no other animal, the pteroid, which helped support the wing.

One Pteranodon fossil has a shark tooth embedded in the neck bones. It was dangerous work snatching fish from the sea!

GLIDING AND FLAPPING

Pteranodon could glide and probably also flapped its wings, at least some of the time. On the ground, it walked on all fours, looking rather ungainly, with its claws on the ground and the long finger with the rest of the wing sticking out behind. To take off, it probably jumped into the air from this position and flapped its wings.

Nothing today walks with the same odd posture as Pteranodon.

Two different body-types are known from Pteranodon fossils, which scientists think are males and females. There are about twice as many probable female Pteranodon fossils as males.

SEASIDE SNACKS

Pteranodon lived by the coast, probably in large colonies on the rocks, and fed mostly on fish. Unlike the early birds, its beak was toothless. It probably reached down for fish while sitting on the water's surface, or even dove from flight as some modern seabirds do. Fossils have been found very far from what would have been the shoreline when the animals were alive, so they could clearly fly far out to sea to feed.

It's possible Pteranodon dove down to snatch up fish from the water, as modern-day pelicans do.

Pteranodon's body was light and short, not taking up much of the animal's length. Its skull, neck, and legs were all separately longer than its torso.

It seems adult Pteranodon grew to very different sizes, but no one knows why.

NOT FEATHERY, BUT FURRY

The body and wings were probably covered with pycnofibers, which are like very fine hairs. These would have helped to keep the animal warm. Pteranodon was probably warm-blooded, so could regulate its own temperature, but for a light animal with a large body, insulation would still be useful.

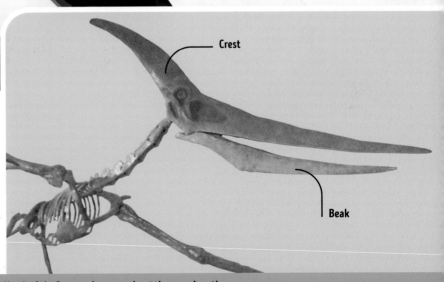

LOOK AT ME!

The enormous crest on Pteranodon's head was made of bone, covered with skin. Despite its huge size, it was very light, as were all Pteranodon's bones. Flying animals need to be as light as possible. The crest perhaps helped to balance the huge, heavy beak, but might also have been brightly colored. A colorful crest could have helped to attract a mate. Males had much larger crests than females, and young Pteranodons had no crest—but they didn't yet need to attract a mate.

Crest

Beak

The crest and beak of the Pteranodon were about the same length.

QUETZALCOATLUS

The largest animal ever to fly in Earth's skies was the giant pterosaur Quetzalcoatlus. The size of a small plane, it, and related species, have been found in North America and Europe. It could probably fly between the two as the landmasses were closer together then than they are now.

NORTH AMERICA

FACT FILE

Name: *Quetzalcoatlus northropi*
Lived: Texas (USA); 70-65 million years ago
Size: Weight 550 lb. (250 kg); wingspan 34 ft. (10.5 m); height 16 ft. (5 m)
Diet: Small land animals
Discovered: In 1971 by Douglas A. Lawson; named in 1975 by Wann Langston

To scale with adult human

SPEEDY FLIER
Once in the air, Quetzalcoatlus might have reached a flying speed of 60 mph (100 km/h), which it could keep up for a few minutes. It could then glide at a cruising speed of 56 mph (90 km/h)—it could keep this up for seven days! That gave it a range of up to 12,117 mi. (19,500 km), meaning it could easily cross the ocean between Europe and North America.

Quetzalcoatlus had a very long, narrow, spike-like beak, without teeth, which it used for snapping up prey.

BEAKY!
Many pterosaurs ate fish, but Quetzalcoatlus's beak and entire body structure weren't well suited to hunting in the water. And no fossils have been found near the coast or even near large inland rivers. Instead, Quetzalcoatlus probably stalked the land, hunting like a modern marabou stork for small animals, such as lizards and baby dinosaurs. It would have swallowed these whole, as it had no teeth.

The marabou stork (left) has a beak much the same shape as that of Quetzalcoatlus.

THE RIGHT SIZE

Quetzalcoatlus was probably as large as a flying animal of this type could ever be. It could possibly work with a slightly larger wingspan, but if its skeleton were much bigger, it could not have remained strong enough while still being light enough to fly. It would also have had difficulty launching itself into the air.

Unlike birds, pterosaurs had much stronger front limbs than back limbs.

The wings of Quetzalcoatlus were flaps of skin stretched between its fingers and its hind legs.

Quetzacoatlus probably used all four limbs to launch itself into the air, pushing off with a leapfrog motion. It was too heavy to launch with just its back legs, like a bird. But we don't know how it landed.

STALKING THE LAND

If Quetzalcoatlus fed on small land animals, it probably hunted them by walking around on all fours over the land. It didn't hunt while flying, just as most birds today don't hunt on the wing. It had a very long neck, another feature it shares with birds such as storks and cranes. However, Quetzalcoatlus had fewer vertebrae in its neck so it was probably not as flexible as the neck of a crane.

Quetzalcoatlus walked on all fours with its knuckles on the ground and its wings folded up behind it from the wrist.

FLIGHT READY

Quetzalcoatlus hatchlings had fully developed wing bones and could probably fly immediately. Modern-day birds are divided into those that are born partially developed, and those that can already stand and feed independently, but none can fly immediately.

STEGOCERAS

Stegoceras could reasonably be called a bonehead. It had a thick cap of bone that sealed its head in an invincible helmet. It was a type of dinosaur called a pachycephalosaur. A bony cap is useful protection for a small plant-eating dinosaur that lived at the same time as some ferocious predators.

NORTH AMERICA

FACT FILE
Name: *Stegoceras validum*
Lived: Alberta, Saskatchewan (Canada), Montana, New Mexico (USA); 76-66 million years ago
Size: Length 7 ft. (2 m); weight 77-88 lb. (35-40 kg)
Diet: Plants, possibly insects
Discovered: In 1898 by Lawrence Lambe; named in 1924 by Charles Walter Gilmore

To scale with adult human

HEAD PUZZLE

Dinosaur experts are still figuring out why Stegoceras had a bony helmet. At first they thought the animals might have head-butted each other when fighting for mates or living space, but the bone might not be strong enough for that, and two rounded surfaces don't make good contact for a tussle. They perhaps butted each other in the flank instead. They might have done the same to try to fend off a predator if their first defense of running away didn't work.

There are no fossilized skin impressions from Stegoceras. It might have had some feather-like strands, as some other small ornithischian dinosaurs did.

The Stegoceras tail was long, slim and very stiff.

Adult

Subadult

Juvenile

Stegoceras was only about the size of a German shepherd dog.

LITTLE FAMILY RESEMBLANCE

Although adult Stegoceras had a dome of bone, infants had a flat bony plate. When fossilized infants were first found, they were thought to be a different species and named Ornatotholus. Much the same happened with the young of Pachychephalosaurus. The very different heads of the young dinosaurs misled scientists into believing they had found two new species in addition to Pachychephalosaurus.

It was clearly not unusual for dinosaurs to change the shape of their bony head ornaments as they matured.

The bone on the head of an adult Stegoceras grew to 3 in. (7.5 cm) thick at its thickest point. Bigger Pachycephalosaurus grew a dome up to 16 in. (40 cm) thick.

Skull domes of pachycephalosaurs, such as Stegoceras, found alone have often been thought to be something completely different, including dinosaur kneecaps!

MORE BONES

Stegoceras and other pachycephalosaurs had extra bone at the rear end. Many of the tendons that would normally attach muscles in the tail to the backbone had hardened into bone, or ossified, giving the dinosaur long, curved segments of bone. How this helped the pachycephalosaurs is unknown. But they are the only land animal to have this feature.

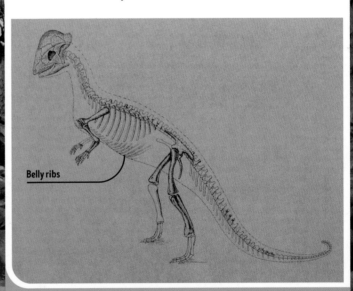

Belly ribs

A drawing from 1924 wrongly placed the ossified tendons in the stomach as "belly ribs."

Stegoceras ran on two legs. Its front limbs were much shorter than its rear limbs.

HEAD BASHING

Pachycephalosaurs are the only dinosaur to have bone directly behind their eyeballs. It might have helped to protect the eyeball from the impact of butting their heads against another animal. Locking ridges in the neck bone also helped to protect the body against the brutal jolts that bashing its head into things would cause.

STEGOSAURUS

Stegosaurus is the most famous of the stegosaurs, a type of ornithiscian dinosaur with plates and spikes along its back, tail, and sometimes shoulders. Found around the world, they came in many shapes and sizes, and Stegosaurus was the largest.

NORTH AMERICA

FACT FILE

Name: *Stegosaurus stenops*
Lived: Wyoming, Colorado (USA); Portugal; 156-144 million years ago
Size: Weight 6,850 lb. (3,100 kg); length 21 ft. (6.5 m)
Diet: Low-growing bushes, ferns, moss
Discovered: In 1877 by Othniel Marsh; named in 1877 by Othniel Marsh

To scale with adult human

ROOF TILES...?

When the first Stegosaurus fossil was found, it was difficult to see how the strange collection of parts should be fitted together. To start with, it wasn't at all clear where the plates (called scutes) on the back should go. One early idea was that they lay flat on the back, overlapping like roof tiles. This gave the animal its name, which means "roof lizard." Another model had the scutes in a single row along the back. In fact, the scutes stood in two rows, not lined up, but alternating on the left and right sides.

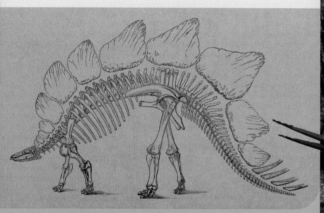

The first drawing by Othniel Marsh showed the Stegosaurus with eight tail spikes (four pairs), rather than four (two pairs).

Every plate, or scute, on the Stegosaurus is different.

The tail spikes were 3 ft. (1 m) long.

A THWACK WITH A THAGOMIZER!

The end of Stegasaurus's tail with its array of sharp spikes was nicknamed "thagomizer." The Stegosaurus could use its thagomizer like a club, causing a nasty injury to any predator that was bothering it.

Its thagomizer helped Stegasaurus fight off enemies.

EARLY SOLAR PANELS?

Stegosaurus scutes look quite spiky, but they're quite thin and not very strong, so were not used for protection. Although the scutes are bony, they were covered with a network of blood vessels, a thin layer of keratin, and then skin. They could have been used to attract a mate, maybe even flushing red with extra blood. They might have helped the animal regulate its temperature. Standing with the scutes facing the sun, the dinosaur could have warmed itself up, the sun heating the blood flowing through them, working rather like solar panels.

Today, animals use different methods to collect energy from the sun. The Namaqua chameleon changes from brown to black to absorb extra heat.

BIG BODY, SMALL BRAIN

Although a Stegosaurus was as long as a bus, its brain was about the size and shape of a bent hotdog. No dinosaur had a huge brain, but this was small even by dinosaur standards.

It was first thought Stegosaurus stood on its hind legs, as its front legs are so short.

STANDING FIRM!

Unlike other dinosaurs that walked on four legs, Stegosaurus held its tail high and its head low. The rear legs were longer than the front legs, so its back slanted downward to the front. This meant its fearsome thagomizer was high enough to give anything that thought of attacking it a good, hard thwack.

STYRACOSAURUS

The name Styracosaurus means "spiked lizard" and that's a good description of it! Styracosaurus had the greatest collection of spikes and horns of any dinosaur. Built like an elephant or rhino, it was heavy and stocky as well as spiky.

NORTH AMERICA

FACT FILE
Name: *Styracosaurus albertensis*
Lived: Alberta (Canada); 75 million years ago
Size: Weight 6,000 lb. (2,700 kg); length 18 ft. (5.5 m)
Diet: Low-growing plants
Discovered: In 1913 by Charles Mortram Sternberg; named in 1913 by Lawrence Lambe

To scale with adult human

PLENTY OF HORNS

Styracosaurus had a lot of sharp horns. On its huge frill, it had four to six long horns as well as two large cheek horns and a horn 24 in. (60 cm) long on its nose. These would have made the dinosaur look very scary to predators, although they were probably better at keeping enemies away than fighting if it came to a battle.

COMMUNICATION BY COLOR

Scientists think the spectacular frill was used for communication—perhaps flushing red with blood as a sign of danger. Styracosaurus probably grazed in herds, so being able to communicate in this way would have helped the herd stay safe. Styracosaurus lived at the same time as the fierce tyrannosaur Albertosaurus. A fit, full-grown Styracosaurus would have been too large for Albertosaurus to tackle, but a warning could save the life of a young or weak individual.

The impressive frill could grow to nearly 3 ft. (1 m) across.

LOST THEN FOUND

The bone bed where the first nearly complete Styracosaurus was found in 1915 was later "lost" for over 90 years. The site wasn't re-found until 2006.

Styracosaurus fed using its parrot-like beak to snip through tough leaves before grinding them up with its rows of small teeth. Extra teeth were stacked behind each tooth that was in use. When a tooth wore out or broke, it was replaced by another.

Each toe ended in an individual horny hoof.

TRICERATOPS

Triceratops's name comes from the Greek for "three horned face," a reference to its most famous features. At up to 8 ft. (2.5 m) long, its huge horned head was one of the largest of all dinosaurs. Triceratops survived right until the end of the dinosaur age, along with its famous rival, T. rex.

NORTH AMERICA

To scale with adult human

BATTLING GIANTS

Triceratops and T. rex clearly had a deadly rivalry. Fossils found show that at least one Triceratops had survived and healed after a T. rex had bitten off one of its horns. There are also remains of Triceratops frills with T. rex toothmarks where they have been bitten. A full-on fight between these massive beasts could have ended in disaster, so they were probably rare.

The horns and frill were probably used in scuffles over mates or ranking. They would also help identify individuals of the same species.

Triceratops had bumpy skin, with hard lumps, or scutes, of different sizes in a patchwork over its body.

One dino expert originally thought Triceratops walked on two legs, and the effort of balancing its heavy skull led to it dying out.

A footprint was 35 in. (90 cm) long. With each stride the Triceratops covered 12 ft. (3.6 m).

ALL ALONE

No complete skeleton of Triceratops has ever been found. The bones that have been found belong to lone individuals, suggesting that Triceratops lived alone for most of the time. They may have moved around in herds for safety.

Triceratops's impressive frill could grow to nearly 3 ft. (1 m) across.

TROODON

The first part of Troodon discovered was a single tooth. It took nearly 100 years to find any bones from this small dinosaur and to identify them as belonging to the same animal. A small feathered theropod, it ran through the undergrowth of the Cretaceous woodlands hunting small animals.

NORTH AMERICA

FACT FILE
Name: *Troodon formosus*
Lived: Alberta (Canada), Alaska, Montana, Wyoming, North Dakota, South Dakota (USA); 77.5-76.5 million years ago
Size: Weight 88 lb. (40 kg); length 6 ft. (2 m)
Diet: Small animals, possibly fruit
Discovered: In 1855 by Ferdinand V. Hayden; named in 1856 by Joseph Leidy

To scale with adult human

CHICKEN BRAIN

Although the brains of dinosaurs don't usually survive, scientists can figure out the size of a dinosaur's brain from the space available in its skull to hold it. Based on this, Troodon had an unusually large brain. Its brain was bigger compared to its body size than that of any other dinosaur, suggesting it was one of the smartest dinosaurs. But even that wasn't very big—or very smart. Troodon was probably about as smart as a modern chicken!

Giant mammoths survived in the coldest regions thousands of years ago.

ADAPTING TO COLD

Troodon grew larger when it lived in colder places, so the largest Troodons are found in Alaska. It's common for animals to be larger in cold environments. Large animals have less surface area for their volume, so they don't lose heat as easily. Animals like giant mammoths and woolly rhinos, which lived much later than dinosaurs, were adapted to living in the cold of the last Ice Age.

EYES FOR HUNTING

Its eyes were set at the front of its head, giving Troodon binocular vision. This meant it could see how far away objects were, which is useful for an animal that needs to hunt. Most plant-eating dinosaurs had eyes on the sides of their head, which gave a wider field of vision. This meant they could spot a predator approaching from the side or behind.

Troodon's tooth was one of the first dinosaur fossils ever found in North America, but wasn't recognized as such. It was thought to come from a lizard.

OUT AT NIGHT

As well as a large brain, Troodon had large eyes. The two go together, as it takes brainpower to work with the information from the eyes. The size of Troodon's eyes suggests that it was trying to see in difficult conditions. Maybe it went out at night or perhaps it needed large eyes because it lived in the far north, where the winters are long and dark.

Nocturnal animals, such as owls, have large eyes that collect a lot of light in the dark.

Troodon had supple, grasping fingers so it could grip wriggling prey.

"WOUNDING TOOTH"

Every Troodon tooth has serrations on each side. Although it looks as though this would be a good tooth for wounding prey, it is similar to the teeth of some plant-eating dinosaurs—so Troodon might have eaten plants as well as other animals.

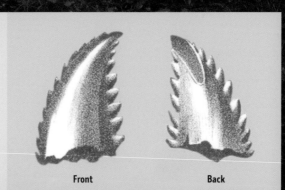

Front

Back

The name Troodon means "wounding tooth."

TYRANNOSAURUS REX

Probably the most famous dinosaur of all is the theropod Tyrannosaurus rex, or T. rex. Its enormous size, terrifyingly ferocious-looking mouth, and survival until the very end of the dinosaur era have made it a megastar among dinosaurs.

NORTH AMERICA

FACT FILE
Name: *Tyrannosaurus rex*
Lived: Alberta (Canada), Montana, South Dakota, Texas (USA); 67-65 million years ago
Size: Weight 15,500 lb. (7,000 kg); length 39 ft. (12 m)
Diet: Plant-eating dinosaurs, carrion
Discovered: In 1902 by Barnum Brown, named in 1905 by Henry Fairfield Osborn

To scale with adult human

BITE SIZED!

T. rex teeth, the largest of any land-based carnivore, had serrated edges, suited to slicing through flesh like a steak knife. But its teeth were not all the same. Those at the front were suited to gripping and tearing and holding on to struggling prey. The side teeth were good for tearing flesh, and the back teeth for slicing it into chunks of a swallowable size. The immensely powerful jaws had the strongest bite of any land animal that has ever lived.

Of its 4 ft. (1.5 m) skull, the jaws took up 3 ft. (1 m).

The thick, muscular tail balanced the weight of the large, heavy head.

Female T. rex have a wider pelvis (hips) than males, allowing space for eggs to form and be laid.

T. rex's closest relatives seem to be Asian. Its ancestors might have invaded North America 67 million years ago, crossing a land bridge from Asia.

CUTE BABIES

T. rex hatchlings were very small. They had to grow incredibly fast to reach their adult size by the time they were 20 years old. A lot of this happened during a teenage growth spurt, when they put on as much as 33–44 lb. (15–20 kg) each week. T.rex hatchlings started about the size of a small turkey covered in feathers. By the time they were adults, they might have had no feathers, or perhaps just a few along the back or on the top of the tail.

Hatchlings were probably covered in downy feathers that made them look fluffy.

Every major T. rex fossil has a different name. The largest, found in 1990, is called Sue, after Sue Hendrickson, who discovered it.

T. rex lived for about only 30 years.

TONS OF FOOD

T. rex hunted plant-eating dinosaurs such as hadrosaurs and Triceratops, but would have happily scavenged any dead dinosaur it found. Needing to eat hundreds of pounds of meat at a time, it couldn't afford to be too fussy. One T. rex would even eat another, but possibly only after it had already died.

The cone-shaped teeth of the T.rex were the size of a large banana and up to 12 in. (30 cm) long.

T. rex's arms were too short to lift food to its mouth. It might have used them to hold on to prey.

UPRIGHT WRONG

Many pictures of T. rex show it standing upright, with its tail pointing down to the ground. In fact, T. rex stood roughly horizontally, with the head and tail in a long line balanced over the massive rear legs. With this posture, it walked at around 3–6 mph (5–10 km/h) and could run at perhaps 10 mph (16 km/h). It didn't need to rely on speed; with excellent eyesight and a keen sense of smell, it could easily find and ambush prey.

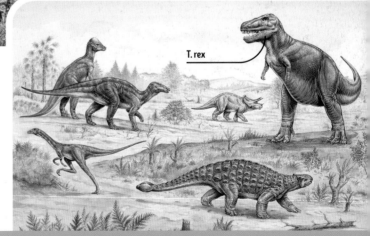

T. rex

Early drawings show T.rex standing upright, like a modern-day kangaroo.

UTAHRAPTOR

As its name suggests, Utahraptor lived on land that is now in Utah, USA, and was a raptor. It was an agile theropod that preyed on the slower dinosaurs in its area. The largest raptor that ever lived, it weighed about five times as much as Deinonychus, or as much as a polar bear.

NORTH AMERICA

FACT FILE

Name: *Utahraptor ostrommaysorum*
Lived: Utah (USA); 139-135 million years ago
Size: Weight 1,100 lb. (500 kg); length 16 ft. (5 m)
Diet: Plant-eating dinosaurs
Discovered: In 1991 by Carl Limoni; named in 1993 by James Kirkland, Robert Gaston and Donald Burge

To scale with adult human

RICH PICKINGS

Utahraptor lived in an area of plains and forests that sometimes flooded, forming bogs. The plains were rich in other wildlife that Utahraptor could prey on, including iguanodonts (like Iguanodon), the ankylosaur Gastonia, and a small sauropod, Moabosaurus, only 33 ft. (10 m) long.

Moabosaurus would have been have been safe unless Utahraptor hunted in packs.

Utahraptor's long, stiff tail would have helped it to balance while fighting prey that might have been quite a bit larger than itself.

Utahraptor was much larger than later raptors such as Deinonychus and Velociraptor. Usually, smaller types of dinosaurs evolve to become larger over time, but Utahraptor reverses the trend.

Powerful back muscles and short but heavy rear legs made Utahraptor strong rather than fast. It could probably deliver a hefty kick.

UNTANGLING UTAHRAPTOR

Because many Utahraptor skeletons have been found, scientists have a range of individuals to compare with each other and similar dinosaurs. Far from being just a larger Deinonychus, the bones showed that Utahraptor was altogether more chunky and robust. In some ways, it's more like a tyrannosaur than a raptor.

Austroraptor

Utahraptor

Microraptor

Velociraptor

Dromeosaurus

Deinonychus

The 2001 discovery gave a more complete picture of the Utahraptor, especially its size compared with other animals.

Its sickle-like claw was up to 10 in. (25 cm) long.

Strong neck and jaw muscles enabled Utahraptor to hold on to prey that struggled in its bite.

FIGHT TO KILL

Utahraptor probably hunted large plant-eating dinosaurs such as iguanodonts by ambushing them. It was not as fast as smaller raptors, but its leg muscles were very powerful and could give a disabling or deadly kick. Its sickle claw and knife-like front claws would then have finished off the animal it caught—or at least held the prey while Utahraptor tore into it with its savage teeth.

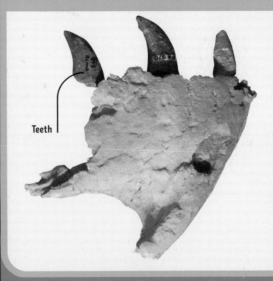

Teeth

These fossilized teeth show they were good for gripping and ripping.

The fearsome Utahraptor used the claws on its front hands like knives to cut prey.

FEATHERED FIEND

Utahraptor probably had feathers, at least as a young animal. These would have helped to keep it warm. When flapping its arms in a struggle with prey, they would also have helped it keep its balance. Utahraptor was certainly too large and heavy to fly.

TRAPPED!

A massive block of rock dug out of a mountainside in Utah in 2001 contains hundreds of Utahraptor bones from animals of different ages. The smallest baby has a jaw bone the size of a penny. The block represents a quicksand trap that the dinosaurs fell into, possibly as a group moving around together, or even separately over a period of time.

SOUTH AMERICA

Dinosaur fossils lurked a little longer underground in South America than North America before coming to the attention of scientists, but it's now a rich hunting ground for paleontologists. Since the 1930s, some of the most important dinosaurs have been discovered in this continent.

ANHANGUERA (pp.54-55)
Brazil

THALASSODREMEUS (pp.70-71)
Brazil

HERRERASAURUS (pp.64-65)
Argentina

ARGENTINOSAURUS (pp.56-57)
Argentina

PRESTOSUCHUS (pp.66-67)
Brazil

GIGANOTOSAURUS (pp.62-63)
Argentina

OLDEST AND EARLIEST

Brazilian paleontologist Llewellyn Ivor Price found one of the earliest of all dinosaurs, the Triassic Staurikosaurus, in 1936. Staurikosaurus lived 233 million years ago. Two more very early dinosaurs soon came to light in Argentina: Herrerasaurus (pp.64–65) was found in 1959, and Eoraptor (pp.60–61) in 1991.

Price was one of the first Brazilian paleontologists.

Some of the largest dinosaurs that ever walked the Earth have been found in South America These are the titanosaurs, such as this Argentinosaurus (p56-57), a giant sauropod up to 130 ft. (40 m) long and weighing 176,000 lb. (80,000 kg). Many exciting discoveries have been made since paleontology took off in South America in the 1980s, and more fossils are still being found.

DEATH OF THE DINOS

One of the most important discoveries to come out of South America is not of how dinosaurs lived, but how their world ended. The Argentinian paleontologist Walter Alvarez, and his father Luis, a physicist, showed in 1980 that a huge asteroid 7 miles (14 km) across crashed into Earth around 65.5 million years ago. The smash would have melted rock and filled the air with poisonous gases and dust that blocked sunlight. This plunged Earth into a period of cold and darkness. Most animals that didn't die immediately would soon have starved as the plants and animals they fed on died. This catastrophe set evolution on a new course— a world without dinosaurs.

The asteroid landed not in South America but nearby, in an area now under the sea off the coast of Mexico. The impact made a giant crater, called the Chicxulub Crater (p.12), and could have created a massive wave up to 1 mi. (1.5 km) high.

DRY AND WINDY

The Ischigualasto Formation in Argentina (shown here) has constant winds so there is little settled soil and the rock is exposed and easily accessible. However, when the earliest dinosaurs lived here, it was a floodplain with active volcanoes, rivers, and heavy seasonal rains. Both Herrerasaurus and Eoraptor fossils have been found here.

ABELISAURUS

Looking rather like a scaled-down T. rex (pp.46–47), Abelisaurus preyed on the plant-eating dinosaurs of Cretaceous Argentina, possibly even tackling sauropods. We don't know much about it, but it gave its name to a group of large theropods also found in other parts of the world.

SOUTH AMERICA

FACT FILE
Name: *Abelisaurus comahuensis*
Lived: Argentina; 83–80 million years ago
Size: Weight 3,000 lb. (1,400 kg); length 23 ft. (7 m)
Diet: Other dinosaurs; possibly sauropods
Discovered: In 1983 by Roberto Abel; named in 1985 by Fernando Novas and José Bonaparte

To scale with adult human

Rough ridges on the skull might have supported a crest made of soft matter that has not survived.

HOLEY HEAD

The skull of Abelisaurus is remarkable for having large holes in it, called fenestrae. Birds have very large fenestrae in their skulls. This makes their skulls light and helps them to fly. Abelisaurus didn't fly, but it had a large head for its body size. It might have been important to have a light skull to help the dinosaur keep its balance. The roof of the skull was quite thick, giving it strength despite the holes.

Nostril

Fenestra

Eye

Its small eye was at the top of one fenestra.

Like other large theropods, Abelisaurus could have had a heavy tail strengthened by chunks of bone.

Abelisaurus

T. rex

Abelisaurus had shorter teeth at the front of the jaw than T. rex.

BITTEN TO DEATH

While theropods like T. rex have a long, narrow snout, Abelisaurus's snout was shorter and more rounded. Even so, much of the skull was given over to the jaws. These held lots of pointed, conical teeth. Abelisaurus had very strong jaw muscles and could give a deadly bite. Because of its short arms, Abelisaurus had to rely on its jaws to hold and kill the animals it ate.

STRANDED ON AN ISLAND

Abelisaurus has given its name to a group of theropods called abelisaurs. Abelisaurs are mainly known from the southern landmass of Gondwana, which is now split between South America, Africa, and Madagascar. Abelisaur fossils are found in all these places, but Abelisaurus itself has been found only in Argentina. This suggests that early abelisaurs spread through Gondwana, but were cut off in different places. When Gondwana split up, the dinosaurs evolved separately into slightly different types.

Abelisaurus has been reconstructed from part of a single skull. Scientists have used information from other dinosaurs to figure out what it looked like.

The short arms would have been no use to Abelisaurus for holding onto a meal that was thrashing around.

Although its teeth were quite short, they were thick and strong and could have held on to a large struggling animal without breaking or coming out.

T. rex had two fingers on each hand but Abelisaurus probably had three.

DINOSAUR HUNTER

An Argentinian dinosaur expert who studied the skull of Abelisaurus, José Bonaparte uncovered evidence of many Argentinian dinosaurs and how they moved around. He discovered and worked on many dinosaurs from South America, including Argentinosaurus (pp.56–57), Carnotaurus (pp.58–59), and Saltasaurus (pp.68–69).

José Bonaparte was one of the leading dinosaur scientists of the last 100 years.

ANHANGUERA

A large pterosaur with scary looking, snaggly teeth, Anhanguera flew over the coastline of what is now Brazil, snatching fish from the water. While its head and neck were very long, its body was quite tiny in comparison.

SOUTH AMERICA

FACT FILE

Name: *Anhanguera blittersdorffi*
Lived: Brazil, Australia, Morrocco; 112–99.5 million years ago
Size: Weight 50 lb. (22.5 kg); wingspan 16 ft. (5 m)
Diet: Fish
Discovered: In 1980s; named in 1985 by Diogenes de Almeida Campos and Alexander Kellner

To scale with adult human

THE "FISH GRAB"

Anhanguera and related types of pterosaurs had a special arrangement of teeth in their beaks, called a "fish grab," which they used to snatch up fish. Their mouth was filled with sharp, backward-pointing teeth that came together to trap fish so they could not escape.

Pterosaurs, like birds and some kinds of dinosaurs, had air spaces in their bones. These made them lighter and helped with flying. Anhanguera and similar pterosaurs had some of the lightest and airiest of all pterosaur bones.

FROM WATER TO AIR

Anhanguera probably didn't have much reason to sit on the water, but it would have ended up on the surface sometimes. To get back into the air, it would have pushed down with its strong wing muscles, with the wings bent, to force its body forwards and into a more upright angle. With a series of hops and flaps, it would have gained enough lift to extend its wings and push off and once again take to the skies.

From a floating position, Anhanguera would push, hop, and flap to become airborne.

The name Anhanguera means "old devil," but it's actually named after a town in Brazil.

Anhanguera was unusual in having crests on both the top and the bottom of its beak.

The wings were well adapted to gliding, like those of modern oceangoing birds.

NOT SO GOOD ON LAND

With much shorter back limbs than front limbs, Anhanguera was clumsy on land. It probably shuffled along, as the front limbs could only take small "steps" without going too far for the rear limbs to keep up. It might also have been able to bound using the front limbs, rather like a person using crutches, putting them well in front and then swinging the back limbs forward.

For an animal with such a small body, Anhanguera had enormous wings—around five times as long as its legs. It didn't need long legs as it spent most of its life in the air.

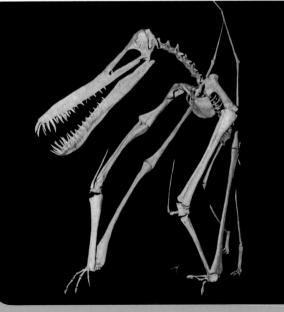

MIGHTY WINGS

To support the large muscles it needed, Anhanguera had a deep chest and a sturdy sternum (breastbone). The wing finger—the extended first finger that forms the final part of the wing—was longer proportionally than on any other pterosaur, providing 60 percent of the wing's length. That's as if you had a finger longer than the rest of your arm!

This skeleton shows that the rear end of Anhanguera was tiny compared to the front.

ARGENTINOSAURUS

The current record-holder for the largest-known dinosaur is the Argentinosaurus, a massive sauropod from Argentina. This mighty dinosaur was nearly twice as long as a railroad car and as tall as a two-story house. It was a titanosaur, one of the largest types of sauropods.

SOUTH AMERICA

FACT FILE

Name: *Argentinosaurus huinculensis*
Lived: Argentina; 96-94 million years ago
Size: Weight 110,000-176,000 lb. (50,000-80,000 kg); length 98-131 ft. (30-40 m)
Diet: Leaves, fruit
Discovered: In 1987 by Guillermo Heredia; named in 1993 by Rodolfo Coria and José Bonaparte

To scale with adult human

MASSIVE!

When the first Argentinoaurus fossil was found, it was mistaken for a lump of fossilized tree as it seemed just too large to be a bone. It was a vertebra (single portion of backbone) and was as big as an adult human.

A single vertebra from Argentinosaurus's massive back.

Large and lumbering, Argentinosaurus probably had a top speed of 5 mph (8 km/h).

Argentinosaurus stood 23 ft. (7 m) tall at the shoulder—about as tall as four adult humans.

A baby Argentinosaurus had a lot of growing to do—it might have taken 30-40 years for an Argentinosaurus to reach its full size.

No Argentinosuarus skull has ever been found. Without teeth to study, experts can only guess at the type of plant food that it ate.

THEROPODS VS SAUROPODS

Remains of Argentinosaurus are sometimes found with fossils of the huge theropod Giganotosaurus, meaning they lived in the same places. Argentinosaurus was far too large for Giganotosaurus to attack and kill alone, but if the theropods hunted in packs, they might have been able to tackle the giant sauropod. As Argentinosaurus also probably lived in herds of up to 20, a hunting scene would have been an impressive sight.

FROM EGG TO ENORMOUS

Despite the huge size of an adult Argentinosaurus, its eggs were probably no more than 12 in. (30 cm) across. This is about as big as it would be possible for a dinosaur's eggs to grow. The mother probably laid 10–15 eggs in a clutch. Most dinosaurs laid lots of eggs, as many young would not survive long enough to reach full size.

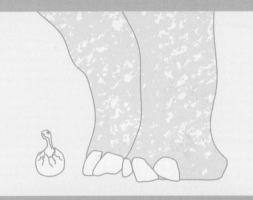

One of the biggest dinosaurs ever came from a tiny egg.

Argentinosaurus had massive hind legs that were each 15 ft. (4.5 m) long.

AS BIG AS A WHALE?

It's not clear whether Argentinosaurus was actually the largest dinosaur. There are other contenders for the record, all of them titanosaurs. Experts don't always have full skeletons that they can compare, so they have to measure the bones they have and do lots of math to decide which dino was biggest. Argentinosaurus might have been the longest animal ever to live, but it wasn't the heaviest. The heaviest animal is still alive today: the blue whale.

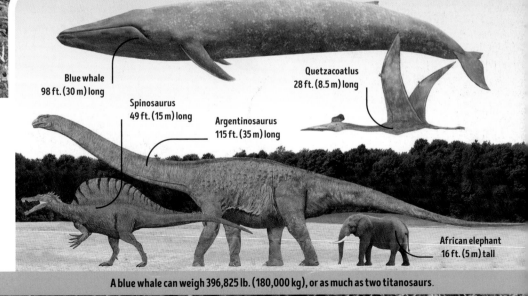

Blue whale
98 ft. (30 m) long

Quetzacoatlus
28 ft. (8.5 m) long

Spinosaurus
49 ft. (15 m) long

Argentinosaurus
115 ft. (35 m) long

African elephant
16 ft. (5 m) tall

A blue whale can weigh 396,825 lb. (180,000 kg), or as much as two titanosaurs.

CARNOTAURUS

If you were a peaceful plant eater living in Argentina 70 million years ago, it would be a bad day when you met Carnotaurus. An abelisaur, it was by far the largest carnivore in the region. It could run fast on huge muscular thighs and was possibly one of the fastest theropods that ever lived.

FACT FILE

Name: *Carnotaurus sastre*
Lived: Argentina; 72-70 million years ago
Size: Weight 2,950 lb. (1,350 kg); length 24-29 ft. (7.5-9 m)
Diet: Meat
Discovered: In 1984 by José Bonaparte; named in 1985 by José Bonaparte

To scale with adult human

NEARLY ARMLESS

Like other abelisaurs, Carnotaurus had extremely small arms. Perhaps if Carnotaurus hadn't become extinct when it did, it would eventually have lost its arms entirely. Like the large early bird Hesperornis (pp.28–29), it might have found its front limbs more of a burden than a benefit and they would slowly have shrunk away to nothing. It had bones for four fingers, but one was longer than the others and ended in a pointed bone.

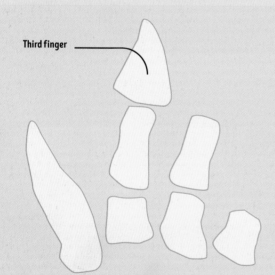

Third finger

Only the third finger had a full set of finger bones and might have looked like a proper finger.

Carnotaurus's legs were long and powerful, meaning it could run fast, probably 40 mph (65 km/h).

WOBBLY SKULL

The bones in your skull are fused together and don't move around. Most animals have a fixed skull like that. But Carnotaurus had a kinetic skull, which means that the bones could move. As the dinosaur took a bite of its prey, its skull bones shifted a little, absorbing the impact of biting down on bone. Some other dinosaurs had kinetic skulls, but none to the same extent as Carnotaurus.

Snakes have a kinetic skull that allows them to open their mouths very wide so they can swallow large prey.

Carnotaurus had scaly skin, like that on lizards, with no evidence of feathers. No babies have been found, so it's still possible that, like many other theropods, the young had some fluff or feathers.

The lower jaw of the Carnotaurus was very small and did not have large jaw muscles. This means that it didn't have a strong bite but it could open its mouth very wide.

The lower part of Carnotaurus's arms were only a quarter the length of the upper part of the arms. Its fingers may have been covered over by the flesh of its hands.

HORNED HEAD

Carnotaurus was the only known theropod dinosaur to have horn-like bumps. Sitting just above the eyes, the bony base of each horn was about 6 in. (15 cm) long. They were possibly further extended with keratin. It is unlikely they were used for defense as Carnotaurus was too large to have enemies. They could have been used in fights for mates, or to show which was the strongest among other Carnotaurus.

Horn-like bumps

The horn-like bumps were where the eyebrows would have been on a mammal.

EORAPTOR

About the size of a large dog, Eoraptor ran around the river valleys of Triassic Argentina. It was one of the very earliest dinosaurs. It lived before the dinosaurs split into the different groups that we now use to divide later dinosaurs.

FACT FILE

Name: *Eoraptor lunensis*
Lived: Argentina; 228 million years ago
Size: Weight 10-20 lb. (4.5-9 kg); length 3 ft. (1 m)
Diet: Plants and small animals
Discovered: In 1991 by Ricardo Martinez; named in 1993 by Paul Sereno

To scale with adult human

LAND OF ARCHOSAURS

In Triassic South America, nearly 230 million years ago, the landscape was dominated by archosaurs, the group of reptiles from which the dinosaurs evolved into species such as Eoraptor. Some archosaurs were very large, and Eoraptor and other early dinosaurs were quite a lot smaller.

Many archosaurs were fierce, crocodile-like animals that walked on two or four legs.

A long tail helped Eoraptor to balance as it ran.

MIX AND MATCH

With curved, serrated teeth in the top jaw and leaf-shaped teeth in the lower jaw, Eoraptor's mouth was a bit of a jumble. The curved teeth were best suited to meat eating, and the leaf-shaped teeth were more common among plant eaters.

It's possible that Eoraptor's top teeth could be seen overlapping its bottom jaw when the mouth was closed.

Long legs and its light weight helped Eoraptor to run fast. It could probably manage 25 mph (40 km/h).

Despite its name, Eoraptor wasn't a true raptor. Raptors evolved quite a bit later. Its rear feet didn't have the giant, raised claw that other raptors had.

THE FIRST DINOSAUR?

Eoraptor is considered a starting point from which other dinosaurs evolved in different directions. It has some features of later theropods, such as clawed, grasping hands and two legs for running fast. But it also has features of prosauropods, such as large nostrils. At different times it's been classed as a theropod, a sauropodomorph (or prosauropod), or as a forerunner of both.

Eoraptor had light, semi-hollow bones that helped reduce its weight.

Its five fingers made Eoraptor different from the theropods that came later. Over the course of evolution, theropods' fingers reduced so that most had three. Some late theropods had even fewer.

NO FUSSY EATER

Its mix of different-shaped teeth suggest that Eoraptor was an omnivore, eating anything it could get. It probably preferred to eat animals, as it takes a smaller amount of meat compared to plant food to give an animal the energy it needs. Being small, Eoraptor probably ate insects and other invertebrates, possibly scavenged dead animals, and maybe stole eggs from other reptiles. It would eat plants such as a horsetails, mosses, and seeds, too.

Moss would have been one of the plants available for Eoraptor to eat.

Like later theropods, Eoraptor had three large toes on its hind feet.

GIGANOTOSAURUS

A towering, fearsome theropod with savage teeth, Giganotosaurus deserves to be called the T. rex (pp.46–47) of South America. It lived in a land of giants: Argentinosaurus lived nearby, and the remains of one of the largest sauropods ever found were discovered in its stomping grounds in 2021.

SOUTH AMERICA

FACT FILE

Name: *Giganotosaurus carolinii*
Lived: Argentina; 99.6 to 97 million years ago
Size: Weight 9,250–30,500 lb. (4,200–13,800 kg) (scientists disagree); length 42 ft. (13 m)
Diet: Meat, probably sauropods
Discovered: In 1993 by Rubén D. Carolini; named in 1995 by Rodolfo Coria and Leonardo Salgado

To scale with adult human

LIGHTWEIGHT OR HEAVYWEIGHT?

When Giganotosaurus was first discovered, it was thought to be even bigger than T. rex by quite a long way. It was put at 56 ft. (14 m) long, while T. rex grew to 39 ft. (12 m). When dinosaur scientists considered it more closely, though, Giganotosaurus turned out not to be quite so big, and perhaps roughly the same length as T. rex. It was perhaps not quite as heavily built as T. rex, and its weight is not known for certain.

Which was the dino king—Giganotosaurus (left) or T. rex?

A full-size model of Giganotosaurus in the main railway station in Frankfurt, Germany, is named "Lady Giga," after the American singer Lady Gaga.

BIT OF A BITE

Giganotosaurus couldn't compete with T. rex's bone-crunching bite. The Giganotosaurus teeth were ideal for slicing through flesh, but its jaw muscles couldn't deliver the brute force of the bite of a T. rex. Instead, Giganotosaurus could have killed by biting repeatedly. Or, with larger prey, it may have waited for the victim to die of blood loss or be so weakened that the dinosaur could begin eating it.

The teeth of Giganotosaurus were all the same type and shape.

SNACKING ON SAUROPODS?

Giganotosaurus lived alongside other dinosaurs, including sauropods such as Argentinosaurus. It could have tackled even these huge dinosaurs by hunting in packs. The related Mapusaurus probably hunted in packs, so Giganotosaurus might have done so, too. A group of seven Mapusaurus have been found together, suggesting the possibility of pack behavior.

SPEEDY OR SLOW?

It's hard to figure out how quickly Giganotosaurus and some other large theropods ran. Although they had large, powerful leg muscles, there might have been other factors that limited their speed. Such an animal couldn't keep its balance above about 30 mph (50 km/h), which sets an upper limit. But it might have been much slower.

Giganotosaurus's brain was smaller than a can of soda, at just 9 fl. oz. (275 ml).

Giganotosaurus's teeth were long, flat, and blade-shaped, with serrated edges, ideal for slicing up its prey.

Like other theropods, Giganotosaurus was a digitigrade—it walked on tiptoes, with its heels off the ground.

PRIDE OF PLACE

An amateur fossil hunter found a leg bone of Giganotosaurus when out driving his dune buggy near Villa El Chocón in Patagonia, Argentina. Professional dinosaur scientists came to excavate the rest of the skeleton. It is now displayed along with the tools used to extract it from the rock and the dune buggy.

The town of Villa El Chocón is rightfully proud of its huge prehistoric resident.

HERRERASAURUS

One of the earliest-known dinosaurs, Herrerasaurus scampered across the floodplains of Argentina in the early Triassic. Far from ruling the world, dinosaurs were scarce at this time. Only around 6 percent of the fossils found in the area where Herrerasaurus lived are of dinosaurs.

SOUTH AMERICA

FACT FILE

Name: *Herrerasaurus ischigualastensis*
Lived: Argentina; 235-230 million years ago
Size: Weight 770 lb. (350 kg);
length 10-20 ft. (3-6 m)
Diet: Meat such as small dinosaurs, small herbivores, and reptiles
Discovered: In 1959 by Victorino Herrera; named in 1963 by Osvaldo Reig

To scale with adult human

PUZZLE PIECES

Many dinosaur fossils are incomplete when they are found, and for a lot of dinosaurs we still don't have a complete skeleton. This makes it difficult to figure out what kind of animal the bones come from. When Herrerasaurus was first found, there weren't enough bones to tell what sort of dinosaur it was, or even to be certain that it was a dinosaur at all.

Experts were better able to tell what Herrerasaurus was like after a complete skull was found in 1988.

Herrerasaurus was discovered when a goatherd called Victorino Herrera trod on a bone while looking after his goats. Its name means "Herrera's lizard."

BECOMING A THEROPOD

Even with a fairly complete skeleton, it's difficult to place Herrerasaurus in the family tree of dinosaurs. Early dinosaurs had not separated fully into the two main groups—bird-hipped and lizard-hipped—that we use to describe later dinosaurs. Herrerasaurus looked quite like a theropod: it ran on two long legs and ate meat. Its legs and forelimbs give experts a clue that Herrerasaurus would develop into the theropods that evolved later.

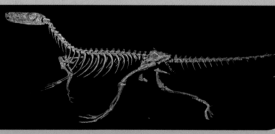

Herrerasaurus's forelimbs were less than half the length of the legs, a feature of later theropods.

A sign of a fast-running animal, Herrerasaurus's legs had much longer shins than thighs. As it walked on just its toes, most of the length of the foot added to the length of the legs.

OPEN WIDE!

The jaws could open very wide, and the bottom jaw had a special joint that allowed it to slide backward and forward. That would have helped Herrerasaurus hold on to a struggling animal, and possibly to rake its teeth over and through an animal, causing serious damage.

24 HOURS

Some animals have rings of bone around their eye sockets. From these, scientists can often figure out the size of the eye and whether the animal was active by day or by night. The bony rings of Herrerasaurus suggest the dinosaur was probably active in short bursts throughout the day and during the night.

Herrerasaurus had a long, narrow skull. Its jaws were packed with sharp teeth with serrated edges, ideal for cutting through flesh.

Three of the Herrerasurus's fingers had vicious, curved claws. At some stage, it may have also had two other fingers that were stumpy and had no claws.

EASY MEALS

Herrerasaurus could have eaten smaller dinosaurs and other reptiles, such as Hyperodapedon. These animals moved slowly, and smaller specimens would have made an easy meal for Herrerasaurus. Although Herrerasaurus was larger than the other early dinosaurs, the main threat was not a dinosaur, but probably something similar to the crocodile-like Sarcosuchus (pp.120–21), 23 ft. (7 m) long and as tall as a human. That might have eaten Herrerasaurus.

Hyperodapedon was a stocky, plant-eating reptile with a beak for biting through tough plant material.

PRESTOSUCHUS

Dinosaurs were not the only animals to live in prehistoric South America. Among the early dinosaurs there stalked giant crocodile-shaped reptiles called rauisuchians. Similar animals lived around the world. One of the largest was Prestosuchus.

FACT FILE

Name: *Prestosuchus chiniquensis*
Lived: Brazil; 231-226 million years ago
Size: Weight 550-660 lb. (250-300 kg); length 26 ft. (8 m)
Diet: Meat, including small dinosaurs and other reptiles
Discovered: In 1938 by Friedrich von Huene; named in 1942 by Friedrich von Huene

AMBUSH HUNTER

Prestosuchus not only looked like a crocodile, it behaved like one, too. Like a modern crocodile, it probably would have lain in wait at a watering hole to ambush and kill animals coming to drink. Unlike a modern crocodile, though, Prestosuchus's prey would be reptiles of different types, including early dinosaurs.

To scale with adult human

This fierce creature had bony plates along its back—though it's hard to think what it needed protecting from!

The vertical position of its legs meant Prestosuchus could move quickly to catch prey.

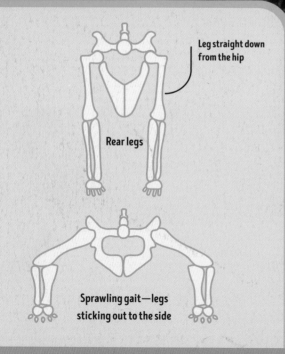

Leg straight down from the hip

Rear legs

Sprawling gait—legs sticking out to the side

LEG WORK

Scientists figured out how Prestosuchus moved from a well-preserved rear leg. Fossils like this show scientists how the muscles were attached to the bones and so how the animal moved. Jurassic reptiles often had a sprawling gait, with the top section of the legs sticking out to the side and then becoming vertical below the knees. Prestosuchus's legs came out from directly under its body.

Prestosuchus's legs were positioned below its body (top), unlike many other non-dinosaur Jurassic reptiles.

TRIASSIC BRAZIL

The area where the fossils of Prestosuchus were found is now grassland, but when Prestosuchus was alive, the region was forest, filled with reptiles and arthropods (jointed invertebrates such as insects). In this type of environment, the archosaurs that dominated the ecosystem eventually gave rise to dinosaurs. But the dinosaurs would not take over for tens of millions of years, and for the time being the land belonged to creatures like Prestosuchus.

Prestosuchus roamed dense forests full of trees, ferns, and mosses.

Prestosuchus had a large, deep skull that held powerful jaws filled with teeth serrated on both edges for slicing and holding on to prey.

LIKE A CROCODILE

Although some rauisuchians walked on their hind legs much of the time, Prestosuchus walked on all fours. It had powerful leg muscles and was a fast runner. Today, crocodiles generally have a sprawling gait, but they can become more upright when they need to run.

A crocodile can pull its legs in under its body to move more quickly.

Backward-pointing teeth made it impossible for captured prey to pull away.

HUNTER AND HUNTED

There were at least 25 species of rauisuchians like Prestosuchus. They were the top predators of their day on land but were not so good in water. When Prestosuchus ventured into a river, it would have been fair game for aquatic, crocodile-like reptiles called phytosaurs.

SALTASAURUS

Saltasaurus might look like just another sauropod, but it had some key differences. It lived on the plains of Cretaceous South America, where the largest sauropods so far known once lived, yet it was small by comparison.

SOUTH AMERICA

FACT FILE

Name: *Saltasaurus loricatus*
Lived: Argentina; 70-66 million years ago
Size: 15,500 lb. (7,000 kg); 39 ft. (12 m) long
Diet: Low-growing plants
Discovered: In 1975-1977 by José Bonaparte, Martin Vince, and Juan Leal; named by José Bonaparte and Jaime Powell in 1980

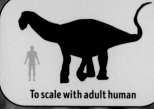

To scale with adult human

LAST OF THE SAUROPODS

In North America, the sauropods died out as the hadrosaurs and ceratopsians took over. However, in South America, sauropods remained dominant and flourished until the end of the age of dinosaurs, and Saltasaurus was one of the last. Some of these final sauropods might have seen the asteroid or comet that crashed into the Mexican coast and caused their extinction.

The object from space that wiped out the dinosaurs left a crater 93 mi. (150 km) wide.

Each large osteoderm was 4-5 in. (10-12 cm) across, and formed a short, cone-shaped spike.

Like other sauropods, Saltasaurus couldn't run. It had to keep its rear legs straight when its weight was on them.

EGGS AND EMBRYOS

A nest site with Saltasaurus eggs has been found in Patagonia, Argentina. Each nest contains around 25 eggs, which are just 5 in. (12 cm) across—a very small size for such a large animal. Scientists believe the site was used by hundreds of Saltasaurus over the years, and this suggests that the dinosaurs may have lived in herds.

Saltasaurus had exceptionally stubby forefeet.

The egg of a Saltasaurus was perfectly spherical.

For a sauropod, Saltasaurus had an unusually short neck.

When Saltasaurus osteoderms were first found, paleontologists thought they were from an ankylosaur or another dinosaur known to have armor.

REACHING THE GROUND

With a fairly short neck, Saltasaurus could not reach for the leaves of tall trees. It had cylindrical teeth with a chisel-like tip. This means it probably ate low-growing plants, such as ferns and cycads. Ferns grew very well in the Cretaceous, providing plenty of food for dinosaurs. Saltasaurus had a large gut, so that it could digest the huge volume of plant matter it had to eat every day.

Many modern types of ferns evolved in the time of Saltasaurus.

Saltasuarus had an extremely wide belly, even for a sauropod.

Many titanosaurs, such as Saltasaurus, lacked the thumb claws of other sauropods. In fact, their forefeet lacked finger bones entirely.

BONY OUTSIDE

Saltasaurus was the first sauropod found to have osteoderms, or bony plates. A few others have been found since. The osteoderms grew within the skin, just below the surface, and gave the dinosaur a protective coat of armor over its back. Many modern reptiles, including lizards and crocodiles, have osteoderms beneath their skin. Saltasaurus had rows of larger oval osteoderms running along its back, and much smaller round or pentagonal ones, called ossicles, in between them.

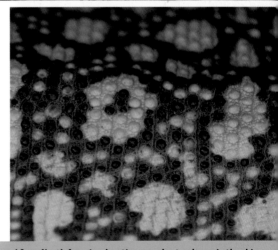

The skin of a modern Gila monster, a type of lizard from North America, has tiny round osteoderms in the skin.

THALASSODROMEUS

Like many other pterosaurs, Thalassodromeus had an enormous decorative crest on its head. In fact, for its size, it had the largest bony crest of any known animal. Another Brazilian pterosaur, Tupandactylus, had a larger crest, but it was made mostly of soft tissue rather than bone.

SOUTH AMERICA

FACT FILE

Name: *Thalassodromeus sethi*

Lived: Brazil; 108 million years ago

Size: Wingspan 5 ft. (4.5 m); height 6 ft. (2 m) when standing

Diet: Reptiles and/or fish

Discovered: In 1983, by various people; named in 2002 by Alexander Kellner and Diogenes de Almeida Campos

To scale with adult human

CHUNKY HEAD

The crest was nearly double the length of Thalassodromeus's skull and about double its height. It began at the tip of the snout and extended well beyond the back of the head, tapering from a thickness of ½ in. (1 cm) at the skull to just ⅟₂₀ in. (1 mm) near the top edge.

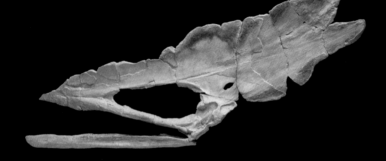

The crest is an extension of the bones of the skull and sticks up and back from the face.

Pterosaurs related to Thalassodromeus had legs about the same length as the front limb, excluding the wing finger. It is likely Thalassodromeus did, too, though no fossils of the legs have been found.

WRONGLY NAMED

The name *Thalassodromeus sethi* means "Seth's sea-runner"—Seth being an ancient Egyptian god. Its crest was thought to look like an Egyptian crown, but the god Seth didn't wear a crown. Even the other part of the name, "sea runner," is wrong. At first, scientists thought Thalassodromeus flew over the sea, trailing its lower jaw to skim for fish, but now they think it probably hunted on land.

Perhaps Thalassodromeus should have been named after the Egyptian god Amun.

RED HEAD

The mighty Thalassodromeus crest was probably covered with a horny material that was the same as the inside of the pterosaur's beak. The crest had a good blood supply and a layer of skin that might have flushed red to attract a mate. Or maybe the crest helped control the animal's temperature.

TOOTHLESS BITE

Thalassodromeus may have stalked the land with its wings folded, or perhaps stood at the edge of the water looking for prey as a modern heron does. It could have stabbed or snapped up fish, lizards, or other small animals, swallowing them whole.

Some modern birds, such as this gray heron, hunt for small animals along riverbanks.

The toothless beak had edges that were narrow and sharp, giving it bladelike cutting surfaces.

FINGERS FOR FLYING

As in other pterosaurs, the hands of Thalassodromeus were wings. It had a very long first finger (wing finger), made up of several bones, which formed the leading edge of the wing. The first bone of the wing finger was much longer than the other bones and made up nearly half the length of the whole finger. The bone at the tip of the wing finger was less than a twentieth of the finger's entire length.

BROKEN BEAK

In 2007, experimenters used a model of Thalassodromeus to test the idea that it fished by skimming the water's surface. The forces acting on the model beak destroyed the equipment, showing Thalassodromeus could not have fed like that. It probably hunted on land. It had strong jaw muscles and would have been able to take quite large prey.

Thalassodromeus's beak was impressive at 27-31 in. (70-80 cm) long.

EUROPE

The first dinosaur fossil known to science was found in Europe, and many more dinosaurs have been found there since. Europe was not only home to dinosaurs, though. The first marine reptiles (plesiosaurs, and ichthyosaurs) were found here, as were the first pterosaurs (flying reptiles).

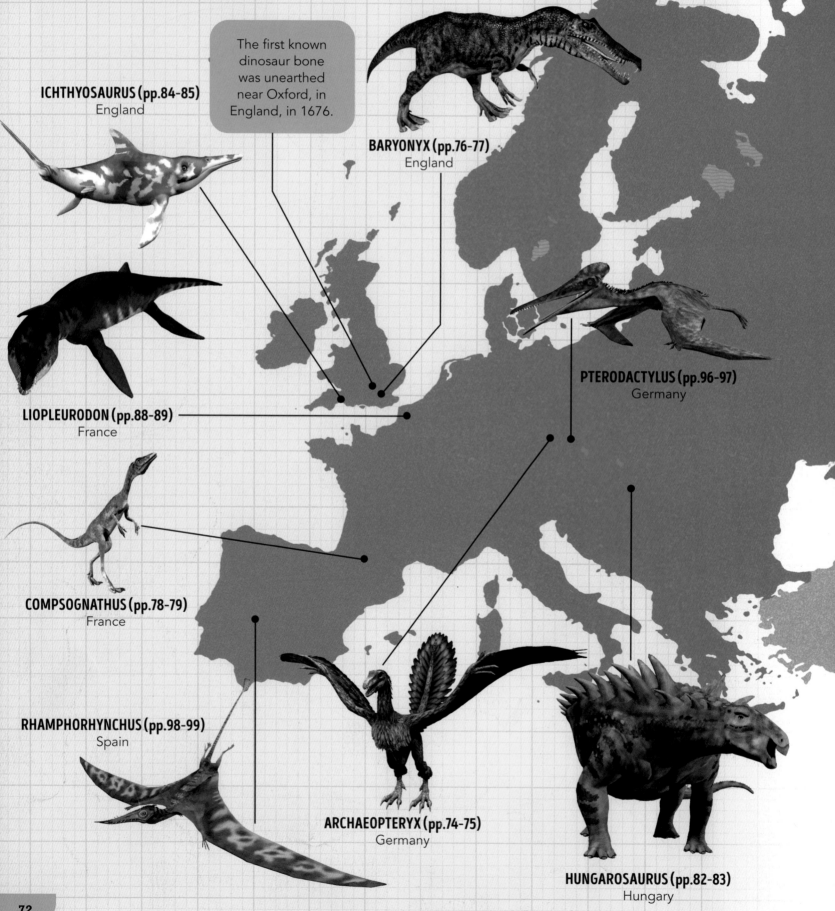

The first known dinosaur bone was unearthed near Oxford, in England, in 1676.

ICHTHYOSAURUS (pp.84-85)
England

BARYONYX (pp.76-77)
England

PTERODACTYLUS (pp.96-97)
Germany

LIOPLEURODON (pp.88-89)
France

COMPSOGNATHUS (pp.78-79)
France

RHAMPHORHYNCHUS (pp.98-99)
Spain

ARCHAEOPTERYX (pp.74-75)
Germany

HUNGAROSAURUS (pp.82-83)
Hungary

WET AND WARM

In the time of the dinosaurs, Europe was a collection of islands and closer to the equator than it is now. Land that is now dry and even mountainous was under a warm sea. Europe was once joined to North America but, as it separated, it also divided into fragments. Animals isolated on small islands evolved independently of their American cousins and even independently of their near neighbors. Europe, like North America, had theropods, sauropods, and ornithischian dinosaurs, but they looked rather different.

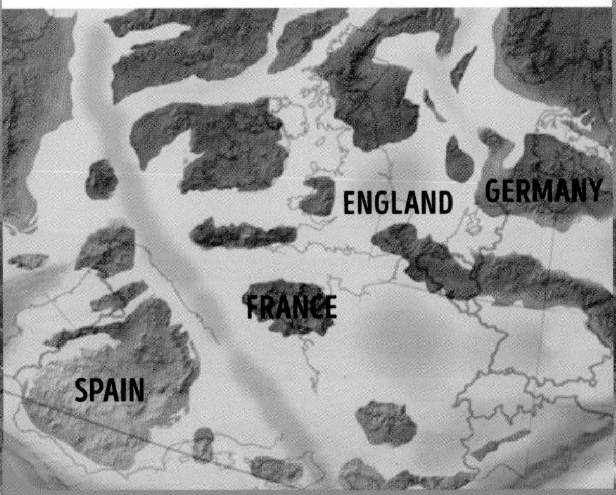

ENGLAND
GERMANY
FRANCE
SPAIN

Much of Jurassic Europe was underwater. Outlines on this map mark the borders of the modern countries. Some of the once-submerged land now has fossils of marine reptiles and seagoing pterosaurs.

FLYING FINDS

Before the discovery of dinosaurs, the fossil of a pterosaur—a flying reptile—was unearthed in Italy in 1748. Pterodacytlus (pp.96–97) was the first of many pterosaurs found around the world. Archaeopteryx (pp.74–75), discovered in Germany in 1860, was a feathered reptile related to both birds and dinosaurs. A full set of dinosaurs, as well as friends from the land, the sea, and the air, had turned up in Europe by the middle of the 19th century.

Animals like Plesiosaurus (pp.94-95) lived in seas around the world, but their fossils are found where old seabed is now exposed inland or at the coast.

FIRST FOSSILS

Marine reptiles were also unearthed in Europe before dinosaurs. The ichthyosaurs and plesiosaurs found by fossil hunter Mary Anning (p.84) on the south coast of England had thrived in the warm sea and were plentiful in the stretch of shoreline where she lived—since renamed the Jurassic Coast (shown here).

IT'S A DINOSAUR

Soon after the marine reptiles, fossils of dinosaurs emerged in England, beginning with Iguanodon (pp.86–87) and Megalosaurus (pp.90–91). The first person to recognize these were part of a group of extinct animals was the English biologist Richard Owen. He coined the term "dinosaur" in 1842, when only three were known, but he saw significant similarities between them. As more dinosaurs were discovered in Europe and North America, it became clear that giant reptiles had once lived all over Earth.

ARCHAEOPTERYX

Archaeopteryx lived at the point at which birds were beginning to separate from their dinosaur ancestors. It had both bird-like and dinosaur-like features. Its discovery, a year after Charles Darwin published his theory of evolution in 1859, supported the idea of organisms changing over time.

EUROPE

FACT FILE
Name: *Archaeopteryx lithographica*
Lived: Southern Germany; 151-149 million years ago
Size: Weight 2 lb. (1 kg); length 19 in. (50 cm)
Diet: Insects, small reptiles
Discovered: In 1860; named in 1861 by Hermann von Meyer

To scale with adult human

Archaeopteryx used its toothed beak to snap up insects and small animals, such as frogs and lizards.

BIRD OR BEAST?
When Archaeopteryx was first described, scientists assumed it was a very early bird. The fossils have visible feathers and wings, and the feet look like bird feet. But there are important differences between the two. Archaeopteryx had feathers, wings, and a beak, but it also had features that modern birds don't have: a long tail with bones, teeth in its beak, and claws emerging from the joint of its wing.

Only one modern-day bird has claws on its wings—the chick of the hoatzin, found in the Amazon rainforest in South America.

The shape of feathers on Archaeopteryx's wings and tail are the same as those of modern birds. This means their feathers were suited to flying.

BALD AND STRINGY
The fossils of Archaeopteryx don't seem to have feathers on the head and upper neck. It might have had thin, downy feathers there, or thin filaments more like hair, or perhaps the neck and head were bald as they are on modern vultures. The body feathers might have been less feathery and more like the stringy feathers of a modern kiwi or cassowary.

Archaeopteryx was first named from a single feather found in 1860.

A vulture has a bald head so feathers don't get in the way when eating prey. Perhaps Archaeopteryx was the same.

FEATHER FINGERS

Unlike pterosaurs, Archaeopteryx did not have a single long "wing finger" that extended to the wing tip. Its arms were more like theropod arms, though longer. The fingers were longer than theropod fingers, but the full length of the wing was provided by feathers.

FOSSIL FEE

The first almost complete fossil of Archaeopteryx was dug up in Germany in 1861. We don't know who discovered it but it was given to a local doctor, Karl Häberlein, as payment of a bill. He later sold it to the Natural History Museum in London for $990 ($117,790 at today's prices).

Rare fossils, such as this Archaeopteryx, can fetch high prices.

Archaeopteryx had a long tail for its size, with bone running all the way to the end, like a theropod's tail.

Scientists have examined Archaeopteryx's melanosomes, the cells in the feathers that produce pigments. Comparing these with the melanosomes of modern birds suggests that Archaeopteryx was mostly black, although it may have had lighter flight feathers, perhaps with black tips.

NO HIGHFLIER

Archaeopteryx could almost certainly fly at least a bit, but it's not clear whether it was better at flapping or gliding. It lacked the strong shoulder muscles needed for long periods of flapping, but to glide it would need to climb trees to launch itself into the air. It didn't have the right claws for climbing trees, and there were not many large trees where it lived.

Archaeopteryx probably flapped a short distance off the ground like modern chickens and pheasants.

BARYONYX

Most dinosaurs lived their lives on dry land, but Baryonyx probably spent at least some time in water, where it hunted for fish. It would have stood in the water by the shore and could probably swim. Baryonyx was the first fish-hunting dinosaur ever found.

EUROPE

FACT FILE

Name: *Baryonyx walkeri*
Lived: England, Spain, Portugal; 125 million years ago
Size: Weight 4,400 lb. (2,000 kg); length 33 ft. (10 m)
Diet: Fish, other reptiles
Discovered: In 1983 by William Walker; named in 1986 by Alan Charig and Angela Milner

To scale with adult human

FISH FOOD

We know Baryonyx ate mostly fish because their remains have been found in the stomach area of Baryonyx fossils. It didn't only eat fish, though. The stomach of one Baryonyx contained parts of a young Iguanodon (pp.8687). It might either have hunted the young animal or fed on it after finding it dead.

Although Baryonyx was identified in 1983, it's possible some of its teeth were first found around 1820, making Baryonyx among the earliest dinosaurs discovered.

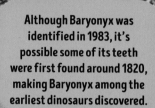

One type of fish Baryonyx ate is called Scheenstia. It was about 29 in. (75 cm) long.

QUITE A CLAW!

The first part of Baryonyx discovered was a giant claw, 12 in. (31 cm) along the edge—and this was from an animal that wasn't yet fully grown!

British plumber and amateur fossil hunter William Walker holds up the giant claw.

EASY FIND

The parts of England where Baryonyx lived were wet and marshy 125 million years ago, so fish would have been easy to find. A mix of fresh water and brackish (slightly salty water) in different streams, pools, and inlets would have had a variety of fish.

HUNT LIKE A BEAR...

Baryonyx might have had several different hunting styles. One method, probably the most common, was to stand on a riverbank, or in the shallows, and spear fish with its claws as they passed. The largest claws were on its thumbs. It could then lift the fish to its mouth, as its front legs were longer than those of most theropods. Or it could just lean over to snatch a fish from the water with its jaws. Bears also do this.

Baryonyx might have caught fish in its mouth, much as bears do today.

Baryonyx had a long, narrow snout, similar to that of a crocodile. Its 95 savage teeth were large and conical with small serrations along the edges. They were suited to gripping rather than breaking up food.

With claws up to 12 in. (30 cm) long on its front limbs, Baryonyx was well equipped to snatch up fish as they swam by.

The giant claw was probably on its thumb.

The angle of its jaws and teeth prevented any fish slipping back out of its mouth once it was caught.

...OR LIKE A CROCODILE?

Baryonyx might have hunted like a crocodile, lying in wait with its snout in the water. Crocodiles have small holes in their skull that enable them to detect changes in water pressure caused by fish moving around. Similar holes in Baryonyx's snout suggest it may have also been able to sense pressure changes. With its nostrils well up on its snout, Baryonyx could breathe with its mouth underwater. If it could detect fish by changes in water pressure, it didn't even need to see its prey, just snatch it in its jaws as it passed.

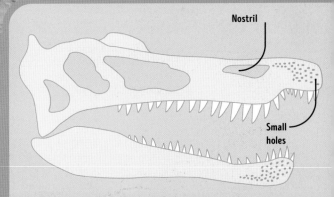

Nostril

Small holes

The small holes in the skull at the front of the snout and the high holes for the nostrils are found in both Baryonyx and crocodiles.

COMPSOGNATHUS

An agile little dinosaur that scampered around France and Germany, Compsognathus was a theropod. Unlike its scarier relatives, it was only about the size of a chicken, with a long tail stuck on the end. It was one of the first nearly complete dinosaur fossils ever found.

OPE

FACT FILE

Name : *Compsognathus longipes*
Lived: France, Germany, possibly Portugal; 145–140 million years ago
Size: Weight 7 lb. (3 kg); length 49 in. (125 cm)
Diet: Small reptiles, insects
Discovered: In the late 1850s by Joseph Oberndorfer; named in 1859 by Johann Wagner

SMALL FOSSILS

The first Compsognathus found was so small experts did not think it was a dinosaur, as they were considered to be large and lumbering in the early days of dinosaur science. A second fossil was found more than 110 years after the first, and these are still the only two known. The second is quite a lot larger than the first, suggesting the first animal was not fully grown when it died.

To scale with adult human

LAST MEAL

We know what Compsognathus ate because the very first fossil found had a small lizard inside—its last meal.

Like other theropods, Compsognathus probably held its neck horizontal most of the time.

Compsognathus had a small head, its jaws packed with tiny, sharp teeth that snapped up lizards that it swallowed whole. Younger animals, too small to swallow a lizard, probably ate insects.

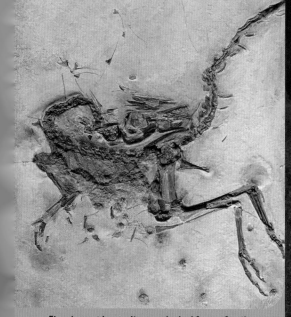

Figuring out how a dinosaur looked from a fossil is difficult, even when it is nearly complete, such as this one of a Compsognathus.

TWO FINGERS OR THREE?

The hands are not intact in either of the Compsognathus fossils, and there has been some disagreement about whether it had two or three fingers, but most experts now think it had three. At one point, it even seemed to have flippers! That would have made it a very odd theropod, but it seemed possible because the fossil was found at the site of an ancient lake. In fact, the flippers belonged to another fossil buried at the same site.

Although it usually held its neck horizontally, Compsognathus could lift its head to look around. This would have been useful for a small dinosaur that might be prey for a larger theropod.

BIRDS AND DINOSAURS

The first Compsognathus was found at the same site as Archaeopteryx. It was similar in size to Archaeopteryx (pp.74–75). The similarities between the two led scientists at the time to suggest an evolutionary link between birds and dinosaurs. The discovery that both animals lived at roughly the same time supported this idea. Now, it is widely accepted that birds evolved from a branch of theropod dinosaurs.

Its long tail helped Compsognathus to keep its balance while running and especially when turning.

While most of the back survives, the end of the tail is missing from both Compsognathus fossils. The tail length is estimated from the shape of the rest of its vertebrae.

Compsognathus ran on two slender rear legs and could run very fast—possibly up to 40 mph (65 km/h).

FEATHERS OR NOT?

Although there is no sign of feathers on either fossil of Compsognathus, many other theropods did have feathers. Its closest relative, the Chinese theropod Sinosauropteryx, had short, fairly basic feathers and so it's possible that Compsognathus had some kind of feathers.

Sinosauropteryx was the first non-bird dinosaur found to have feathers.

EUROPASAURUS

We think of sauropods as huge. For example, Diplodocus (pp.24-25) was 85 ft. (26 m) long and weighed 44,092 lb. (20,000 kg), while the giant titanosaur Argentinosaurus (pp.56-57) was even longer and weighed at least 110,229 lb. (50,000 kg). Europasaurus looks puny in comparison.

EUROPE

FACT FILE

Name: *Europasaurus holgeri*
Lived: Germany; 155.7-150.8 million years ago
Size: Weight 1,100-1,550 lb. (500-700 kg); length 9 ft. (6 m)
Diet: Plants
Discovered: In 1998 by Holger Lüdtke; named in 2006 by P.M. Sander, Octavio Mateus, Thomas Laven, and Nils Knötschke

To scale with adult human

SMALL ISLANDS, SMALL ANIMALS

Today, Europe is a continental landmass with a few islands dotted around. But in the Jurassic period, sea levels were higher and much more of Europe was underwater, the rest being broken into islands. It's common for species isolated on islands for a long time to gradually become smaller, as there is limited food available to them, and this is what happened to sauropods in Europe.

Much of modern Europe was underwater at the time Compsognathus was alive.

SHRUNKEN COUSINS

While their American relatives still had vast tracts of land to stomp through, and more food to eat, the European sauropods, such as Europasaurus and Magyarsaurus, were restricted to small islands with less food. They couldn't move between islands. The result was sauropods that looked as though they had shrunk. However, Europasaurus skeletons fall into two very different sizes, with some being 35–50 percent larger than the others. It's possible that males and females were different sizes.

Diplodocus was about four times as long as its European cousin, Europosaurus.

After lying safely in the ground for 154 million years, many of the recovered bones of Europasaurus were destroyed or damaged in a fire in 2003, including some of the vertebrae.

BONE CHANGES

A small sauropod skeleton could come from a young sauropod that just hadn't reached its full size when it died. But experts can tell whether a fossil is of a fully grown or juvenile animal because bones change as an animal ages. Extra layers of bone are laid down, which can be counted like tree rings to calculate the animal's age at death. This tells us that Europasaurus was as small as an adult human.

Some of Europasaurus's neck vertebrae are missing, so we can't be sure how long its neck was.

We have no skin fossils from Europasaurus, but similar sauropods had hexagonal scales 1 in. (2.5 cm) across on the upper body and much smaller scales, ¼ in. (2-4 mm) across, on the underside.

OLD HEAD

In most animals, bones in the skull that are separate in a young animal fuse together as it grows older. The young usually have larger eyes for the size of their heads, and bigger holes for their eyes. Europasaurus, though, kept large eye holes and gaps in its skull even as an adult.

The big eye holes and gaps in the skull of an adult make it look like that of a youngster.

CARNIVORE CARNAGE!

Experts have found fossilized footprints of theropods in the rock layers above where Europasaurus is found. They believe the sea level fell and opened a land bridge to an island where theropods lived. The meat eaters could then cross this bridge and make a meal of Europasaurus, whose small size left them with few defenses. This may have contributed to the extinction of Europasaurus.

Europasaurus may have been wiped out in quite a short time, probably by an invasion of carnivorous theropod dinosaurs.

HUNGAROSAURUS

Hungarosaurus was a nodosaur, a subgroup of the ankylosaurs. Nodosaurs and other ankylosaurs evolved from an ancestor that also produced stegosaurs, the other group of dinosaurs that generally came equipped with defensive spikes and bony plates.

EUROPE

FACT FILE
Name: *Hungarosaurus tormai*
Lived: Hungary; 86.3–83.6 million years ago
Size: Weight 1,550 lb. (700 kg);
length 15 ft. (4.5 m)
Diet: Low-growing plants
Discovered: In 2000 by András Torma;
named in 2005 by Attila Ősi

To scale with adult human

SPIKES AND PLATES

As a nodosaur, Hungarosaurus belonged to a group of robust, tank-like animals such as Ankylosaurus (pp.18–19). Nodosaurs appeared suddenly in the early Cretaceous and quickly diversified, so that there were soon lots of different types. Their bony plates and sharp spikes were a good defense against predators, as the success of nodosaurs around the world proves.

The stomach contents of a fossilized nodosaur show that it ate soft plants and ferns, but not cycads, conifers, or hard twigs.

LOOKING GOOD

We have a very good idea of what a nodosaur like Hungarosaurus would have looked like in life because the best-preserved dinosaur fossil found so far is of a nodosaur. A Borealopelta, a nodosaur from Canada that lived about 110 million years ago, had been naturally mummified (dried out) after it died before becoming fossilized, so the animal's fossil looks much as it did in life. It even shows its protective coloring, reddish-brown on top and paler underneath, so that it was camouflaged in the undergrowth.

The large gut needed to cope with the vegetation Hungarosaurus ate. Plants generally have less nutritional value than meat, so a plant eater needs to eat more than a meat eater.

The soft tissue of the Borealopelta had dried out and been preserved, rather than rotting away, before it became fossilized.

BIG AND LITTLE BITES

Clearly, Hungarosaurus's bony armor and spikes protected it from the bite of large predators—but it was probably also protected from biting insects. Fossilized midges and other bugs found in the same place as the Hungarosaurus fossil show that biting bugs could have troubled an animal with thinner, unprotected skin.

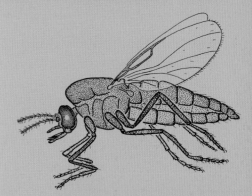

The midge Leptoconops hasn't changed much since the time of Hungarosaurus.

Their bony plates, called osteoderms, locked together to form an armored covering.

The front of the mouth had a hard, sharp beak for snipping through plants. Further back in the mouth, leaf-shaped teeth chopped them up a bit to speed digestion in the gut.

TAIL ENDS

Although many of the later ankylosaurs had a heavy tail club as part of their defensive armory, Hungarosaurus probably did not—certainly, none has been found. But the dinosaurs possibly did form a club! The fossils of four individuals have been found together, which suggests that they might have lived in groups for safety.

Hungarosurus had a wide body that was low to the ground, which made it difficult for a predator to unbalance it, and perhaps roll it over to attack its vulnerable belly.

GROUND-LEVEL EATING

Nodosaurs helped scientists figure out when North America and Europe split apart. Different nodosaurs each side of the Atlantic from around 113 million years ago show sea levels had risen and separated the animals. Hungarosaurs lived on the floodplains of the low-lying islands of central Europe. The ground was open, flat, wet, and fertile, leading to lots of low-growing plants that Hungarosaurus could eat.

ICHTHYOSAURUS

Although Ichthyosaurus looks rather like a tuna or perhaps a dolphin, it was neither a fish nor a mammal but a seagoing reptile. As such, it needed to breathe air (like a dolphin does) and so could not stay underwater all the time. It was completely adapted to living in the sea, though, and could never venture onto land.

EUROPE

FACT FILE

Name: *Ichthyosaurus communis*
Lived: Belgium, England, Germany, Switzerland, Indonesia; 201-194 million years ago
Size: Length 10 ft. (3 m)
Diet: Fish and cephalopods
Discovered: In 1811 by Mary Anning; named in 1821 by William Conybeare and Henry De la Beche

To scale with adult human

EARLY FIND

The first Ichthyosaurus fossil was found by Mary Anning in 1811, when she was just 12. Anning was a talented fossil hunter and a self-taught expert paleontologist who made a living selling the fossils she found in the cliffs of Lyme Regis, England. The Ichthyosaurus was the first complete fossil she found, before people even recognized that some animals had gone extinct.

Mary Anning walked the seashore with her dog hunting for fossils.

A bone behind the eyeball helped to protect the eye from high pressure in deep water.

A narrow snout packed with needle-sharp teeth was suited to catching fish and cephalopods like squid.

The bulbous, smooth body and pointed nose gave Ichthyosaurus a streamlined shape for zipping through the water.

SPEEDY SWIMMER

A closely related ichthyosaur called Stenopterygius is believed to have been capable of speeds up to 60 mph (100 km/h), and Ichthyosaurus could probably have come close to that, too. A strong tail pushed the animal through the water, and a streamlined shape reduced drag. The tail had bones in only the lower fin. This was a continuation of the backbone.

Fossilized ichthyosaurs often have an outline of their soft tissues preserved, so we can see their shape and not just their bones.

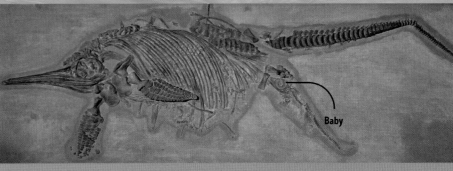

Baby

This is a fossil of a mother Ichthyosaurus giving birth to a baby.

Ichthyosaurus had a large, fleshy fin on its back that had no bones inside.

Ichthyosaurus was descended from land-living ancestors. The rear legs had shrunk to small flippers, much shorter and less powerful than the front flippers.

FAR AND WIDE
Although fossils of Ichthyosaurus are mostly found in Europe, they probably swam all over the world. There was less difference in the water temperature in different areas than there is now. They are found in Europe because the right conditions for fossilizing them existed there, and now, millions of years later, the rock that contains their fossils is near the surface.

IGUANODON

Iguanodon has been confused with another dinosaur, mistaken for an entirely different animal, and had body parts put in the wrong places. This is excusable, as dinosaurs were unknown at the time: Iguanodon was one of the first ever discovered.

EUROPE

To scale with adult human

JUST ONE TOOTH

The first find was a single tooth discovered in England by either Gideon Mantell, a country doctor, or his wife, Mary Ann. Most paleontologists dismissed the tooth as belonging to a fish or a rhinoceros, but one noticed it looked like a very large iguana tooth. Mantell named the tooth's owner Iguanodon.

The similarity between Iguanodon and an iguana doesn't go far beyond the teeth—the iguana is a very different animal.

Iguanodon had rough skin with a pebbly texture.

GETTING IT WRONG

The first recreation of the Iguanodon was completely wrong! The animal was given legs of about equal length, and a long tail that dragged on the ground. And it was thought to be a massive 39 ft. (18 m) long. It was given an iguana's four-legged posture, too. In later interpretations, it was shown standing on its hind legs with its tail as support, a position it couldn't have managed without breaking its stiff tail.

Although better than the first image, this Iguanodon from 1905 is still very wrong.

MISTAKEN IDENTITY

In the early days of dinosaur science, scientists had no idea how many different dinosaurs there were. As new dinosaurs were discovered, many were classed as the same types as those first found, Iguanodon and Megalosaurus (pp.90–91). Since the 1980s, many of the early finds have been separated into different types. Even the original Iguanodon found by Mantell has been renamed Therosaurus.

ALL THUMBS

The discovery of a second fossil in 1834 gave scientists more to work with, including a large spike. This was at first put on the nose as a horn, but we now know it to be a giant thumb spike. Plant-eating Iguanodon used it to pull on branches and perhaps to defend itself against predators.

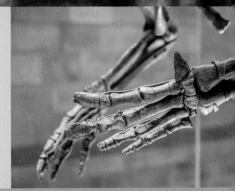

The thumb spike sticks out at a right angles to the fingers and, unlike a claw, it's straight.

DINNER IN A DINOSAUR

Iguanodon was included in a series of supposedly life-size sculptures of dinosaurs and other extinct animals made for the gardens of Crystal Palace in London in 1854. They were the first dinosaur sculptures anywhere in the world, though they don't match current ideas of what the dinosaurs looked like.

A banquet took place in the mold used to make the Iguanodon on New Year's Eve, 1853, before the dinosaur models were complete. The thumb spike is visible on the nose (left).

Iguanodon was only the second dinosaur named. Megalosaurus was the first.

LIOPLEURODON

With a head more than 3 ft. (1 m) long and a mouth packed with teeth, each the length of a banana, Liopleurodon was a true sea monster. It was a pliosaur, a marine reptile that breathed air but lived its life entirely in the water.

FACT FILE
Name: *Liopleurodon ferox*
Lived: England, France, Germany, possibly South America; 166-155 million years ago
Size: Weight 22,000-37,500 lb. (10,000-17,000 kg); length 23 ft. (7 m)
Diet: Fish, squid, other marine reptiles
Discovered: In 1873; named in 1873 by Henri-Émile Sauvage

To scale with adult human

BIG AND BIGGER

Pliosaurs were the top predators of the Jurassic seas. The jaws of Liopleurodon took up a fifth of the animal's entire length and had a very powerful bite. One skull that measured just over 5 ft. (1.5 m) long suggests that Liopleurodon could grow to 24 ft. (7.5 m). Even so, Liopleurodon wasn't the largest pliosaur. Another European pliosaur, which for a long time was called Predator X, could have been nearly 42 ft. (13 m) long. It has now been named *Pliosaurus funkei*. Such huge creatures had nothing to fear except, perhaps, an even larger pliosaur.

Liopleurodon's snaggly, forward-pointing teeth made it hard for prey to escape.

SPEEDY HUNTER

Pliosaur limbs evolved to be efficient paddles as they spent more and more time in the water and less on land. Liopleurodon could move fast and accelerate quickly, which was important for catching fast-swimming prey. It had a very good sense of smell, so it could locate food from far away and then speed towards it before it swam off.

Liopleurodon's teeth were up to 8 in. (20 cm) long and were deeply rooted in its jaw so that they wouldn't be yanked out by struggling prey.

TOO BIG

Liopleurodon got a reputation for being even bigger than it was when a British television show described it as being 82 ft. (25 m) long. There is no evidence that Liopleurodon could ever grow to that size.

SCARY GNASHERS

This picture shows the creature's variety of different-sized teeth. They had a combination of sharp, fang-shaped, and snaggly teeth. The first identified fossil of Liopleurodon was a single tooth. Its name means "smooth-sided tooth."

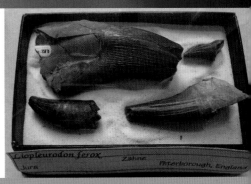

Liopleurodon had different-sized teeth, but even its smaller ones were thick and strong.

Recent studies on the tail bones of plesiosaurs suggest that some had a small, vertical fin at the tip of the tail. It is unknown whether or not Liopleurodon had such a fin.

Both sets of flippers were used to push Liopleurodon forward, forcing water out of the way with powerful strokes.

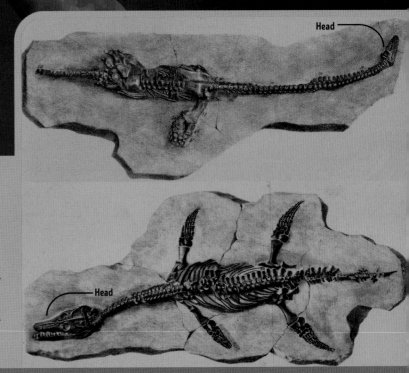

Head

PLESIOSAUR OR PLIOSAUR?

Plesiosaurs and pliosaurs were both marine reptiles that had evolved from reptiles that originally lived on land. They both breathed air and gave birth to live young. They were closely related but had quite different shapes. Pliosaurs, like Liopleurodon, had a very large head on a short neck, a stocky body, and a short tail. Plesiosaurs had a much smaller head on a much longer neck. They were more streamlined and often had a longer tail.

Head

The large head makes it easy to spot a pliosaur (bottom), while the plesiosaur had a longer neck.

MEGALOSAURUS

The first dinosaur ever discovered, Megalosaurus was a large meat eater that roamed Jurassic England. It was the discovery of Megalosaurus that led to the creation of the word "dinosaur," meaning "terrible lizard"—a bit unfair as they weren't all terrible and they weren't lizards!

EUROPE

FACT FILE
Name: *Megalosaurus bucklandii*
Lived: England; 170-155 million years ago
Size: Weight 2,200 lb. (1,000 kg); length 19 ft. (6 m)
Diet: Meat
Discovered: In 1676; first named by William Buckland in 1824; renamed in 1827 by Gideon Mantell

To scale with adult human

DINOSAUR OR GIANT?
The very first dinosaur part we know of anyone finding was almost certainly a bit of Megalosaurus's leg bone. It was found in a limestone quarry in Oxfordshire, England, in 1676 and was taken to Robert Plot at the University of Oxford. Plot identified it as part of a leg bone. This was long before anyone knew about dinosaurs, and Plot thought it was a bone from a long-lost race of giant humans.

From the few parts of Megalosaurus's skull that survive, the animal seems to have had a large head for its size compared to other theropods.

No foot bones survive from Megalosaurus, but it would have walked on three toes.

TERRIBLE LIZARDS
In 1815, the geologist William Buckland got hold of more fossils from the same area as Plot's leg bone and wondered what animal they were from. The French scientist Georges Cuvier correctly identified the bones as coming from a giant reptile of some unknown kind, rather like a lizard. His mention of lizards would later lead to the English biologist Richard Owen inventing the word "dinosaur" in 1842.

Nearly 200 years after bones were discovered by William Buckland, the Royal Mint in Great Britain issued a commemorative coin in color that shows Megalosaurus.

ODD IDEAS

Early experts had some odd ideas about what Megalosaurus looked like. They put it on all fours, like a giant lizard, with a snout rather like a crocodile's, packed with teeth. Early claims that it was 50 ft. (15 m) long were way off, too. By 1900, ideas had changed. Experts believed Megalosaurus walked on its hind legs and had small front limbs. But they thought its tail dragged on the ground and it walked in an upright posture. In reality, Megalosaurus walked on its rear legs, held its body, tail, and head in a fairly straight horizontal line, and had shorter front limbs than rear limbs.

This model in Crystal Palace Park, London, UK, from 1854 incorrectly gave Megalosaurus a slightly humped back, feet that looked like those of a large mammal, and a long tail that drooped to the ground.

Many later dinosaur finds were wrongly classed as types of Megalosaurus but have now been renamed.

There was probably a small crest above the hips. The neural spines growing from the vertebrae were longest here.

The top predator of its region, Megalosaurus had nothing to fear.

OOPS!

Early ideas about dinosaurs had them as sluggish, bulky creatures that were always fierce. A drawing of Megalosaurus and Iguanodon (pp.86–87) fighting, drawn in 1863, shows Iguanodon (a peaceful plant eater) biting Megalosaurus using meat-eater teeth. The horn on Iguanodon's face was really a spike on its thumb, but put in the wrong place by scientists who did not yet fully understand dinosaurs.

DINOS BY THE BEACH

The region where the fossils of Megalosaurus have been found was once by the sea, and Megalosaurus fossils lie near those of marine animals. Megalosaurus might have hunted inland, like other theropods, but also snacked on animals like plesiosaurs resting in shallow water, or scavenged on sea creatures washed up on the beach.

Megalosaurus (right) and Iguanodon (left) as imagined in 1863.

PLATEOSAURUS

Plateosaurus lived long before the large sauropods of the Jurassic. It's a sauropodomorph, which means "sauropod-shaped." Sauropodomorphs include the sauropods and their ancestors. Plateosaurus wasn't as large as most later sauropods, and it walked on two legs, while sauropods walked on four.

EUROPE

FACT FILE
Name: *Plateosaurus engelhardti*
Lived: Germany, Switzerland, Austria, Greenland; 214-204 million years ago
Size: Weight 1,300-4,000 lb. (600-1,800 kg); length 16-33 ft. (5-10 m)
Diet: Cycad, conifers, club ferns
Discovered: In 1834 by Johann Friedrich Engelhardt; named in 1837 by Hermann von Meyer

To scale with adult human

TEETH FOR TOUGH FOOD

With broad, leaf-shaped teeth and strong jaw muscles, Plateosaurus's mouth was suited to cutting through and mashing tough plant material such as conifers and cycads. It would have broken down food with its teeth a bit more than later sauropods, who simply gulped it down whole and relied on their gut to break it up.

These jaws gave Plateosaurus a powerful bite.

Some adult Plateosaurus were nearly twice as big as others. It's possible their size was limited by the availability of food.

The oldest known Plateosaurus was 27 years old when it died.

IT'S A HERD LIFE

More than 100 Plateosaurus seem to have died together. Their fossils were found in a quarry near the village of Trossingen, in Germany. Perhaps they became trapped in boggy areas while looking for food. A heavy animal struggling to free itself from mud will sink rather than escape. No young animals have been found among the large number of adults, but they were probably light enough to avoid sinking into the mud.

Many fossils of Plateoasurus survive.

The neck was long and flexible, and the narrow head was three times as long as it was tall.

Plateosaurus fossils have been recovered from below the seabed, off the coast of Norway. (It wasn't sea at the time Plateosaurus was living.)

FOSSILIZED TODDLER

A fossil of a young Plateosaurus found in Switzerland in 2015 has been named Fabian. The toddler is 6 ft. (2 m) long and weighed about 88–132 lb. (40–60 kg)—a pretty big toddler! Its body proportions were the same as those of its parents, while many young dinosaurs had quite different proportions from their parents.

Unlike many other dinosaur babies, Fabian looked like a scaled-down version of its parent.

Plateosaurus had claws on its hands that it could use for grasping branches and twigs while feeding. It might also have used them for slashing at any predators that tackled it.

Evidence from its bones suggests Plateosaurus was warm-blooded.

PLESIOSAURUS

One of the first marine reptiles ever discovered, Plesiosaurus emerged from the rock as a complete skeleton. It was found in the cliffs of the Dorset coast (England) by Mary Anning in 1824 (p.84), soon after dinosaur fossils began to appear (although Plesiosaurus is not a dinosaur).

EUROPE

FACT FILE

Name : *Plesiosaurus dolichodeirus*

Lived: Sea around England; 199-175 million years ago

Size: Weight 200 lb. (90 kg); length 11 ft. (3.5 m)

Diet: Fish, squid

Discovered: In 1823 by Mary Anning; named in 1824 by William Conybeare and Henry De la Beche

To scale with adult human

IN AND OUT OF WATER

Plesiosaurs were reptiles and had to visit the surface of the water to breathe. The discovery of a fossilized pregnant plesiosaur, as well as pregnant fossils of related animals, show that plesiosaurs and other marine reptiles gave birth to live young. The young would have had to go straight to the surface of the sea to take their first breath.

The leg bones that any four-legged animal has, one in the thigh and two in the lower leg, were short and crammed into the top end of the rear flipper of the Plesiosaurus. Most of the flipper's length was extra foot bones.

Pictures often show plesiosaurs holding their head out of the water or curling their neck around, but they almost certainly couldn't do either. Their neck muscles needed the support of water.

EYE BONES

Plesiosaurs, like ichthyosaurs and some other marine reptiles and even birds, had a ring of bone behind the eyeball. Sitting in the eye socket, this helped to support the eye. It probably allowed Plesiosaurus to dive without the increased water pressure changing the shape of its eyeball and either damaging it or affecting the animal's vision.

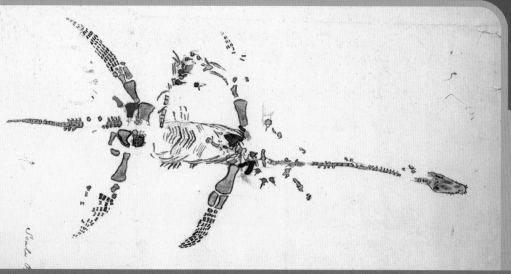

Mary Anning's drawing of Plesiosaurus

FAKE OR REAL?

When Mary Anning found the first Plesiosaurus, it was considered so strange that some people thought the fossil was a fake. Even the greatest fossil expert of the day, Georges Cuvier, doubted it was real. A meeting was called to discuss it, but as a woman, Anning wasn't invited—women scientists were given little recognition or respect at the time. Eventually, the experts agreed the animal was real.

FINGER COUNT

Although their hands were fused into a flipper, Plesiosaurus had more bones in each "finger" than land animals. The longest Plesiosaurus finger had nine bones (your fingers have four bones each).

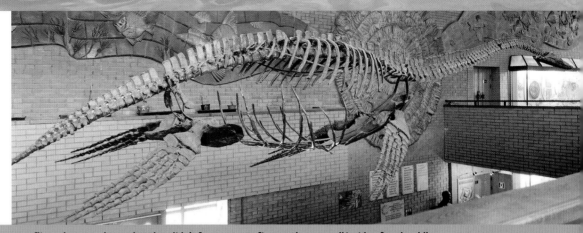

Each Plesiosaurus flipper has many bones, but they didn't form separate fingers: they were all inside a fused paddle.

GOTCHA!

Plesiosaurus fed on fish and mollusks, including squid-like creatures, snails, and shellfish. Its teeth were narrow, conical, and pointed, and they overlapped the edges of the mouth and interlocked so that prey could not wriggle free.

Plesiosaurs are often shown with a humped back, but fossilized plesiosaurs are straight.

Plesiosaurus was not able to move on land at all. Its stiff and inflexible flippers were suited to moving in water.

FLYING WITH FLIPPERS

Experiments using a virtual plesiosaur suggest Plesiosaurus flapped its flippers up and down, rather like flying underwater, with the front flippers doing most of the work. The rear flippers might have given the animal an occasional burst of speed.

Head

The tips of a Plesiosaurus's paddles trace long shapes in the water as it swims.

PTERODACTYLUS

People often talk of "pterodactyls," but there is no creature that scientists call "pterodactyl." The name comes from Pterodactylus, the first pterosaur to be discovered. One of the smaller pterosaurs, it had a wingspan of only about 39 in. (100 cm), so about the size of a macaw.

EUROPE

FACT FILE

Name: *Pterodactylus antiquus*
Lived: Germany; 150-144 million years ago
Size: Weight 10 lb. (4.5 kg); wingspan 3 ft. (1 m); length 35 in. (90 cm)
Diet: Insects, small animals, fish
Discovered: In 1784 by Cosimo Alessandro Collini; named by Georges Cuvier in 1809

To scale with adult human

EARLY PUZZLE

Pterodactylus was the first pterosaur anyone had come across, so no one knew what to make of it. It was found before dinosaurs had been recognized, and before experts agreed that some animals become extinct, and so a fossil could be of something no longer living. At first, some scientists thought Pterodactylus was a kind of bat, or something between a bat and a bird. There were even suggestions that it lived in the water and was either an aquatic reptile or an amphibian, and that the wings were actually flippers.

The first Pterodactylus fossil was dug up where Archaeopteryx (pp.72-73) was found. They would have flown in the same skies at the same time.

NO GROWN-UPS

Scientists can tell from the bones of an animal whether it is an adult, and no adult Pterodactylus has ever been found. The smallest died in its first year and had a skull just ½ in. (1.5 cm) long, while the largest lived to their third year and had skulls over 4 in. (10 cm long). The youngest only had 15 teeth, whereas the largest and oldest had 90 teeth.

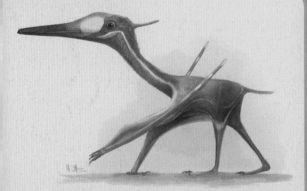

Pterosaur hatchlings are called "flaplings."

SMALL TO GIANT

Early pterosaurs were fairly small and, like Pterodactylus, had a wingspan of only 3 ft. (1 m) or so. Later, some grew to be giants—the largest flying animals Earth has ever seen.

Pterodactylus had a throat pouch. It might have scooped up a pouchful of water, then let the water drain out of its beak, leaving any fish trapped.

Older Pterodactylus had narrower teeth than the youngsters, and the teeth at the front of the mouth were larger.

Pterodactylus means "wing finger."

FROM TAIL TO TAIL-LESS

Pterodactylus was not the earliest pterosaur by a long way. The first pterosaurs were small animals with long tails, no head crests, and stocky snouts with two different types of teeth. Animals such as Eudimorphodon, and later Dimorphodon, ran over the ground or flew through the skies of Europe around 200 million years ago.

Dimorphodon lived in Europe 190 million years ago. It might have hunted small animals on land.

DROWNED!

The reason so many young Pterodactylus survive as fossils might be because they drowned. Pterodactylus floated well, but a young Pterodactylus with weak wing muscles might have struggled to get airborne and out of the water.

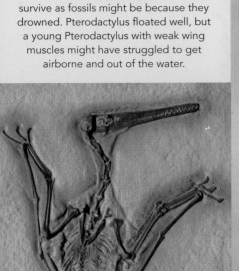

Most Pteradactylus fossilss are found in areas that were swampy.

SWOOP, SWIM, OR STALK?

Pterodactylus could fly and walk, and probably also swim. Its large feet would have been good for spreading its weight over the soft, muddy ground at the water's edge. They might even have helped it to paddle while sitting on the surface of the water. The animal may have walked and swum in the same way as some modern wading birds, snatching small animals from shallow water while standing or floating.

Modern wading birds like this snipe hunt in shallow water.

RHAMPHORHYNCHUS

A pterosaur with a long tail, Rhamphorhynchus probably flew over the coasts of Europe in large numbers, perhaps like modern seagulls. Unlike seagulls, though, their beaks bristled with long needlelike teeth that meshed together to give maximum grip on their slippery prey.

EUROPE

FACT FILE
Name: *Rhamphorhynchus longicaudus*
Lived: Germany, Portugal, Spain, England, Tanzania; 150.8-148.5 million years ago
Size: Wingspan 6 ft. (2 m); length 3 ft. (1 m)
Diet: Fish, squid, perhaps insects when young
Discovered: In 1825 by Georg Graf zu Münster; named in 1847 by Christian Erich Hermann von Meyer

To scale with adult human

CHILDREN AND ADULTS

For a while, it seemed there were several different species of Rhamphorhynchus, but then in 1995, scientists noticed that most were the same animal but at different ages. It turns out that Rhamphorhynchus changed quite considerably as it grew up. Young Rhamphorhynchus had shorter and blunter jaws than the adults, but longer, thinner, sharper teeth. The adults probably had shorter, stronger teeth that were more robust and less likely to break while holding struggling prey.

Rhamphorhynchus teeth were sharp, snaggly, and scary looking.

Some pterosaurs, such as Pterodactylus (pp.96-97), had very short tails, just a slight extension of the backbone. Others, like Rhamphorhynchus, had a long tail that swept out behind them.

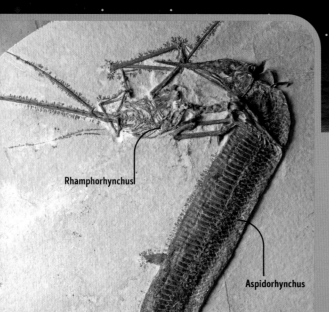

Rhamphorhynchus

Aspidorhynchus

TWO FOR ONE

Several fossils of Rhamphorhynchus show it apparently caught in the jaws of a large fish called Aspidorhynchus. This suggests that the fish deliberately looked for Rhamphorhynchus as a meal, and sometimes both were killed in the struggle.

This fossil captures the moment a large fish (right) catches a Rhamphorynchus by its wing.

FLYING BY NIGHT

The size of the bones at the back of its eye sockets suggests that Rhamphorhynchus had large eyes and so was possibly nocturnal. This would give it the advantage of being out hunting while other pterosaurs were asleep, so reducing the competition for food.

Males and females possibly looked a bit different. Rhamphorhynchus with larger and smaller heads are found in roughly equal numbers.

The upturned, sharp beak had no teeth at the very end and seems suited to snapping fish from the sea, probably while Rhamphorhynchus was swimming.

Rhamphorhynchus ate fish and cephalopods such as squid.

CHANGING TAILS

Rhamphorhynchus's tail had a feature at the end called a vane that changed as it grew. It began as roughly oval, then became diamond-shaped, and ended up triangular. The tail vane stood vertically, like a fish's tail, not horizontally, like a dolphin's tail.

Its tail would have helped Rhamphorhynchus balance as it swooped through the air.

GETTING WARM!

It's not clear whether pterosaurs were warm-blooded or cold-blooded. A cold-blooded animal needs an outside heat source to warm its body. If Rhamphorhynchus was cold-blooded, it's been suggested that it might have used warmth from the ground that had been heated by the sun.

Rhamphorhynchus possibly rested in the sun on the ground or rocks.

AFRICA

The huge continent of Africa now has a landscape of parched deserts, open grasslands, tropical rainforest, volcanic mountains, and fertile floodplains, home to a huge variety of animals. It might have been the same in the time of the dinosaurs. Large areas were covered with lush forest and swampy floodplains. They could have supported many different types of dinosaurs. Dinosaur fossils were first found in Africa in the 1840s.

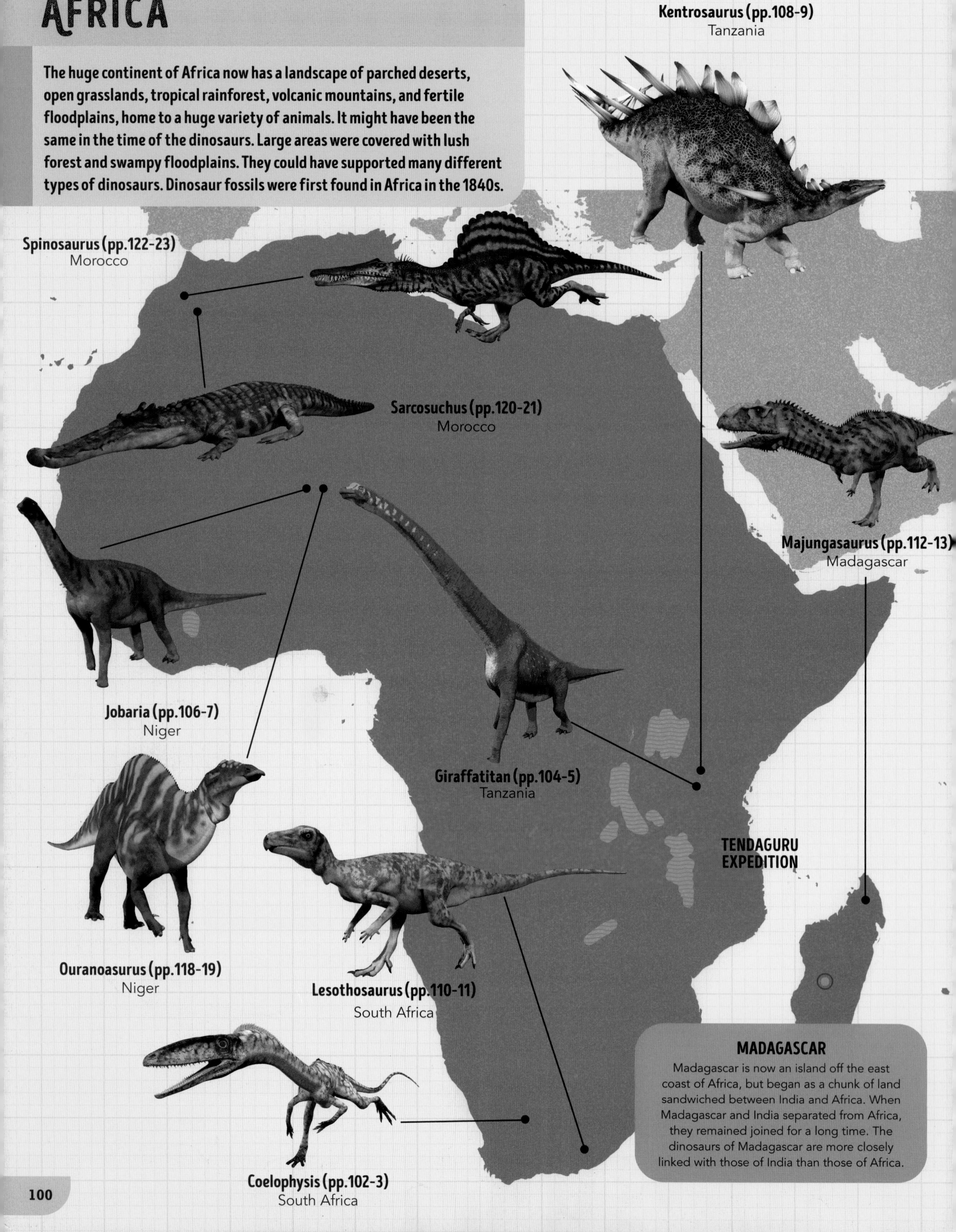

Kentrosaurus (pp.108-9)
Tanzania

Spinosaurus (pp.122-23)
Morocco

Sarcosuchus (pp.120-21)
Morocco

Majungasaurus (pp.112-13)
Madagascar

Jobaria (pp.106-7)
Niger

Giraffatitan (pp.104-5)
Tanzania

TENDAGURU EXPEDITION

Ouranoasurus (pp.118-19)
Niger

Lesothosaurus (pp.110-11)
South Africa

MADAGASCAR

Madagascar is now an island off the east coast of Africa, but began as a chunk of land sandwiched between India and Africa. When Madagascar and India separated from Africa, they remained joined for a long time. The dinosaurs of Madagascar are more closely linked with those of India than those of Africa.

Coelophysis (pp.102-3)
South Africa

HUNTING FOR AFRICAN DINOSAURS

Most early expeditions to look for fossils were organized by museums based outside Africa. One of the most important was a German expedition to Tendaguru, in Tanzania, in 1909–1912. The site was buried deep in the forest. The fossils had to be dug out and packed up using simple tools and carried by skilled porters on foot to the coast. From there, they were shipped to Germany to be studied.

Moving heavy dinosaur fossils from the forest to the coast during the Tendaguru expedition was hot and difficult work that required great care to avoid damaging the fossils.

A PLACE FOR DINOSAURS

Africa began the age of dinosaurs, connected to South America on one side and Antarctica and India on the other. There are lots of similarities between the dinosaurs of these continents because the early dinosaurs could walk between them. The Tendaguru expedition revealed that the climate of Jurassic Tanzania was partly dry, but with seasonal rains. A coastal area had shallow lagoons and tidal flats, and inland areas had many plants that dinosaurs could eat.

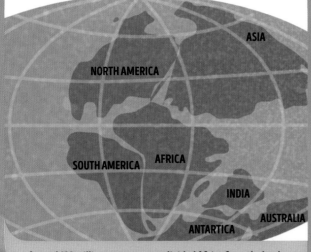

Around 120 million years ago, sea divided Africa from the lands it had been joined to.

MODERN FOSSIL HUNT

Today, more African countries search for their fossils themselves. The dinosaurs can stay in Africa, being investigated by African paleontologists and displayed in African museums.

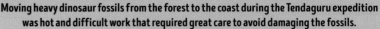

Dinosaur skeletons greet visitors at the Transvaal Museum of Natural History in Pretoria, South Africa.

ABUNDANT LIFE

The Elliot Formation in South Africa (shown here) was once home to dinosaurs including Massospondylus (pp.114–15), Plateosaurus (pp.92–93), and Coelophysis. At the time the dinosaurs lived here, in the late Triassic and early Jurassic, the area had rivers, lakes, and floodplains. There was abundant life, and many types of dinosaurs, crocodile-like animals, and even early types of mammals have fossilized and been discovered here. Volcanoes in this region caused the land that is now Africa to separate first from South America and then from India and Madagascar, finally leaving the African dinosaurs stranded.

COELOPHYSIS

The early dinosaur Coelophysis was a theropod that skittered through the forests of South Africa and Zimbabwe and was also common in North America. With long legs and sharp teeth, it evolved into a speedy, savage hunter that would grow large enough to terrorize later dinosaurs.

AFRICA

FACT FILE
Name: *Coelophysis bauri*
Lived: New Mexico, Arizona (USA); South Africa, Zimbabwe; 209-201 million years ago
Size: Weight 55 lb. (25 kg); height 10 ft. (3 m); length 3 ft. (1 m)
Diet: Reptiles, carrion
Discovered: In 1881 by David Baldwin (and his mule); named in 1889 by Edward Drinker Cope

To scale with adult human

SPEEDY SPRINTER
Coelophysis was built for running. Like later theropods, it had much longer legs than arms, and it ran on two feet. Its legs were much thinner than those of later theropods, though. It was also very light, with hollow bones. Indeed, its name means "hollow bones." Being light helped it to run at speeds of 25–30 mph (40–50 km/h).

Its long, thin tail helped Coelophysis to balance its head and neck as it ran and turned.

Coelophysis had the bones for four fingers on each hand. But one finger stayed buried in the hand, so only three had flesh and formed proper fingers.

PACK HUNT
Coelophysis may have hunted in packs. Groups could have tackled large animals by working together, just as wolves or lions do today. The discovery of thousands of Coelophysis bones buried together in a quarry in New Mexico, USA, supports this idea.

ALL THE BETTER TO SEE YOU WITH...

Scientists can figure out the size of an animal's eyes by looking at the space in the skull that the eye sat in (the eye socket). The position of its eyes gave Coelophysis good depth perception, which meant it could accurately judge how far away a prey animal was. Coelophysis ate quite small animals. These are harder to spot and track than large, slow, plant-eating dinosaurs, so the dinosaur needed good eyesight.

Coelophysis could probably see as well as modern birds that have eyes of a similar size and position, such as this peregrine falcon (left) and sparrow.

Coelophysis came in two adult sizes. Either males or females were much bigger than their companions—but we don't know which.

Its long, narrow snout had razor-like teeth. The size of its teeth were suitable for feeding on lizards and other small reptiles.

BONE SECRETS

Dinosaur scientists have to be cautious figuring out behavior from fossils. Even when a lot of bones are found together, this doesn't always mean the animals lived as a pack. A large number of dinosaurs of the same type could have a come together during a disaster, such as a flood. Or they might have died at different times at the same watering hole, maybe months or years apart, yet be buried in the same place.

This mass of bones could mean that Coelophysis formed packs or that lots of individual animals were caught in a sudden flood.

GIRAFFATITAN

Like its namesake the giraffe, Giraffatitan towered over the animals around it. If you want to see a really large dinosaur, this is the best bet. Although a few others were larger, including Argentinosaurus (pp.56–57), Giraffatitan is the largest for which we have found most of a skeleton.

AFRICA

To scale with adult human

FACT FILE

Name: *Giraffatitan brancai*
Lived: Tanzania; 145–150 million years ago
Size: Weight 106,000 lb. (48,000 kg); length 82 ft. (25 m)
Diet: Leaves
Discovered: In 1909–1912 by Werner Janensch; named *Brachiosaurus brancai* in 1914 by Werner Janensch; renamed *Giraffatitan brancai* in 1991 by George Olshevsky

YEARS OF MISTAKES

For 80 years, Giraffatitan was thought to be the same animal as Brachiosaurus. When the two were finally compared, nearly every bone turned out to be different! In the past, some scientists believed that Giraffatitan lived in the water, as its body was too large to be supported on land. They thought its nostrils were on the top of its head, acting like a snorkel as it lay under the water. In fact, it couldn't have breathed underwater because the water pressure would have been too great.

EARLY MEASUREMENTS

Figuring out the weight of an extinct animal is difficult. The highest estimate for Giraffatitan's weight is 171,958 lb. (78,000 kg)—more than five times the lowest estimate of 33,069 lb. (15,000 kg). Earlier scientists figured out the volume of the dinosaur by measuring how much sand or water a scale model of it displaced, then multiplying the volume by a rough estimate of the dinosaur's density. There are much better methods today.

Giraffatitan (top) and Brachiosaurus skulls show the difference in size.

A Giraffatitan fossil is the tallest mounted skeleton in the world, at 39 ft. (12 m). It is in the Museum für Naturkunde in Berlin, Germany.

COMPUTER MEASUREMENTS

Today, scientists use measurements of bones and computer models of a dinosaur's body structure to calculate its volume and weight. These calculations also take into account the weight-saving air sacs in the bones. We don't know how fat or skinny dinosaurs were, though, so there will always be a bit of guesswork involved.

HOT OR COLD?

Scientists have long disagreed about whether Giraffatitan and similar dinosaurs were warm- or cold-blooded. A warm-blooded animal would have needed a lot of food—more then 397 lb. (180 kg) a day! It would have needed only about half as much food if it were cold-blooded, but it would have taken 100 years to grow to full size.

Many sauropods held their neck and tail horizontally as they moved about, but Giraffatitan could also hold its neck up straight and reach right to the treetops to feed.

As a large, warm-blooded animal, an elephant spends up to 18 hours a day eating over 220 lb. (100 kg) of food.

Giraffatitan's front legs were much longer than the rear legs. This raised its shoulders and made its back slope downward from the shoulders toward the tail.

BONE CARRIERS

The dinosaur was discovered by German paleontologists during an expedition to Tendaguru in Tanzania in the early 20th century. It revealed a lot about the environment in which dinosaurs lived 165–130 million years ago. The climate was partly dry, but with seasonal rains. There was a coastal area with shallow lagoons and inland areas with many plants that dinosaurs could eat. The area was quite like the places in North America where large numbers of dinosaurs lived and hunted each other.

The Tendaguru fossil-hunting expedition uncovered many huge dinosaur bones, including these Giraffatitan bones.

JOBARIA

A large sauropod found in the Sahara desert, Jobaria once wandered through the Jurassic landscape of Niger in northern Africa. Although the area is now dry, it was a floodplain with rivers weaving through it when Jobaria lived there.

AFRICA

FACT FILE

Name: *Jobaria tiguidensis*
Lived: Niger; 167-161 million years ago
Size: Weight 48,500 lb. (22,000 kg); length 69 ft. (21 m)
Diet: Leaves from trees
Discovered: In 1997 by Paul Sereno; named in 1999 by Paul Sereno

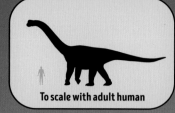

To scale with adult human

BITTEN!

One fossil of a young Jobaria has tooth marks on its ribs. It was bitten by an animal tall and fierce enough to tackle a young sauropod. The most likely culprit seems to be Afrovenator, a theropod similar to Megalosaurus and the main predator where Jobaria lived. Teeth from Afrovenator were found at the site (though probably not from the actual animal that bit Jobaria).

Predators such as this Afrovenator would have hunted young Jobaria.

A SIMPLE BEAST

Jobaria had a simpler body in many ways than other sauropods from the same time. These features make it seem like an early type of sauropod. Scientists call animals that appear early in the evolution of a new type "basal." Refinements and adaptations collect as the animal evolves. Jobaria has several features of basal sauropods but was not especially early, which is a puzzle.

Most of Jobaria's bones have been found, leaving only 5 percent of its skeleton unknown.

Paul Sereno stands in front of a model of a rearing Jobaria fossil.

BALANCING BULK

To defend itself or its family, Jobaria may have reared up on its hind legs. To find out whether this was possible, paleontologist Paul Sereno studied the largest African elephant in captivity. He found that the elephant could stand on its rear legs, even though it usually carries most of its weight on its front feet. Jobaria carried most of its weight on its rear feet so could have reared up more easily than an elephant.

The footprint made by a rear foot was one and half times the area of a front footprint, suggesting most of Jobaria's weight was carried at the back.

SHORT HEAD

Jobaria had a blunt, rounded snout with strong, broad, spoon-shaped teeth. It probably used these to browse on the leaves of medium-height to tall trees. Sauropods with a very large hole in the skull behind the nostril are called macronarian sauropods. In Jobaria, the hole is even larger than is usual in macronarians.

A plant eater doesn't need as strong a skull as a predator and can have large holes to keep its skull light.

Jobaria had a short neck for a sauropod, with only 12 neck vertebrae. Some sauropods had as many as 19.

NAMED FOR A MONSTER

The name Jobaria is taken from a monster called Jobar, that features in Tuareg folklore. The Tuareg are a nomadic people who live in the area where Jobaria's fossil was found. Stories about the creature were created to explain the massive bones found sticking out of the ground in the area—so Jobaria was named after the legendary creature and the creature was invented to explain Jobaria!

The front legs were quite short compared to the back legs.

FEW FINGERS

Sauropod digits, equivalent to fingers, are arranged in a column inside the flesh of the foot, apart from one claw sticking out at the side. In many other animals, including you, they are splayed out as separate fingers. The single claw might have been used for scraping at the ground, perhaps to make a shallow nest.

Like many other sauropods, Jobaria probably had only one claw on each front foot.

KENTROSAURUS

The small stegosaur Kentrosaurus has an appropriate name: it means "spiked lizard." The dinosaur probably had more spikes than any other stegosaur. It lived in a tropical or subtropical area with rainy and dry seasons.

FACT FILE

Name: *Kentrosaurus aethiopicus*
Lived: Tanzania; 156-150 million years ago
Size: Weight 2,200 lb. (1,000 kg); length 16 ft. (5 m)
Diet: Ferns, leaves, moss, cycads, conifers
Discovered: In 1909 by a German expedition; recognized as a stegosaur in 1910 by Werner Janensch; named in 1915 by Edwin Hennig

To scale with adult human

FULLY PROTECTED

Two lines of plates extended from Kentrosaurus's head and down its back, but about halfway along the back they changed to fierce spikes that would have given a potential attacker pause for thought. The plates, like those of Stegosaurus (pp.40–41), were thin and not much use for protection. They had a rich blood supply and might have been used to attract a mate by flushing with color.

Although fearsomely spiky, Kentrosaurus was only about the height of a cow.

The 40 or so spikes along the back end of Kentrosaurus continued to the end of the tail, and were up to 24 in. (60 cm) long.

Kentrosaurus had much longer rear legs than front legs. This means its tail was further off the ground and perhaps at a better height for thwacking its spikes at attackers.

UP AND DOWN FEAST

Kentrosaurus could probably rear up on its hind legs briefly. It might have used this trick to reach higher leaves. Most of the time, it probably ate low-growing ferns, horsetails, and club mosses, but if it reared up, it might also eat from bushes and low trees. Conifers were plentiful where it lived, and it probably fed on them, too.

Horsetails are a very old type of plant that still grow today.

TURN AND SWIPE

Because its tail was extremely flexible, Kentrosaurus could swing it hard enough for the end to strike an attacker at 30 mph (50 km/h)! That's fast enough to kill a theropod if it struck it on the head. It could also turn quickly to whip around and swipe an attacker from the side.

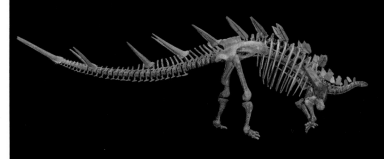

The tail of the Kentrosaurus was more than twice as long as its body.

Kentrosaurus had long spikes on either its shoulders or hips, but experts aren't sure which.

WALL OF SPIKES

Kentrosaurus might have lived in herds. To date, at the Tendaguru site in Tanzania where Kentrosaurus fossils are found, 1,200 bones from around 50 individuals have been uncovered. A herd of Kentrosaurus could have arranged themselves as a wall of spiky tails that would have been hard for a predator to break through.

Kentrosaurus had a tiny brain, about the size of a walnut. It was one of the least intelligent dinosaurs.

BEAK AND TEETH

Kentrosaurus's beak was toothless at the front and used for snipping through stems and twigs. It had just a few chewing teeth further back. These teeth would not have had much impact on tough leaves, and Kentrosaurus swallowed its food in large chunks. The food was then ground down in its belly.

Female Kentrosaurus were probably larger than the males.

LESOTHOSAURUS

Lesothosaurus was one of the earliest ornithischians—the group of dinosaurs that later included some of the heavy armored animals, such as ankylosaurs and ceratopsians. Lesothosaurus was completely unlike them, though. It was small, slender, and ran fast on its back legs.

AFRICA

FACT FILE

Name: *Lesothosaurus diagnosticus*
Lived: Lesotho, South Africa; 199-189 million years ago
Size: Weight: 11-20 lb. (5-9 kg); length 6 ft. (2 m)
Diet: Plants, small animals
Discovered: In 1963-4 by a University College, London expedition; named in 1978 by Peter Galton

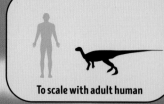

To scale with adult human

BIRD HIPS

Early in dinosaur history, two different groups emerged, which are now divided by the shape of their hips. Ornithischian dinosaurs like Parasaurolophus and Triceratops had "bird hips." Many of them could walk on two legs sometimes, at least when young, but most walked on four legs as adults.

Animals with hips like those of birds are called bird-hipped or ornithischian dinosaurs.

Its teeth show us that Lesothosaurus was probably an omnivore, able to eat both plants and animals.

LIZARD HIPS

Sauropods and theropods were all "lizard-hipped" dinosaurs. Most sauropods walked on all fours and theropods on two legs. Lizard-hipped theropods look more like birds than the bird-hipped dinosaurs. Birds even evolved from the lizard-hipped theropods! But the style of hips that birds have evolved separately—it's just coincidence that ornithischians have the same kinds of hips as birds.

Some animals had hips like those of lizards and are called lizard-hipped or saurischian dinosaurs.

SNIP AND SHRED

Like later ornithischians, Lesothosaurus had a beak for snipping through plants and small leaf-shaped teeth for shredding leaves. But it also had 12 fangs in its upper jaw near the front of its mouth. These suggest that it could eat meat as well as plants. It might have fed on small animals, such as Megazostrodon, when soft-leaved plants were not available.

The mammal-like Megazostrodon, just 4 in. (10 cm) long, might have made a snack for Lesothosaurus.

SINGLE SITE

Lesotho is a small country that is entirely surrounded by South Africa. It's the only place Lesothosaurus has been found. At the time Lesothosaurus was living, floodplains and winding rivers were giving way to a drier environment, but with some flash-floods. Today, Lesotho is cooler than much of South Africa.

LESOTHO

SOUTH AFRICA

Lesotho would have been even further inland when Lesothosaurus lived there.

HEAVY AND NOT SO HEAVY

There is a lot of variety in later bird-hipped dinosaurs. Lesothosaurus looks more like the lighter ornithischians, such as the hadrosaurs and pachycephalosaurs. Heavier bird-hipped dinosaurs, such as the stegosaurs, ankylosaurs, and ceratopsians, were stocky and low to the ground, and walked on four legs.

Lesothosaurus was a very early ornithischian that lived before the split between the two types of hip had taken place.

All the lighter bird-hipped dinosaurs had shorter front legs than back legs, but Lesothosaurus's front legs were much shorter.

SPEEDY ESCAPE

Theropods ran quickly to chase after the animals they ate, but Lesothosaurus probably used considerable speed to escape being eaten itself. It was light, with very long legs. Hollow bones helped to keep its weight down. It had large eyes, which would have helped it to keep a lookout for the movement of predators on the plains or in the undergrowth.

MAJUNGASAURUS

A giant flesh-eating theropod, Majungasaurus was the apex predator—the top meat eater, with no rivals—in the tropical forests and woodlands of Cretaceous Madagascar. It was an abelisaur, the same type of dinosaur as Abelisaurus (pp.52-53), which lived in South America just a few million years earlier.

FACT FILE
Name: *Majungasaurus crenatissimus*
Lived: Madagascar; 70-66.8 million years ago
Size: Weight 2,400 lb. (1,100 kg); length 23 ft. (7 m)
Diet: Other dinosaurs, possibly even sauropods
Discovered: In 1896 by an unknown French army officer; named in 1955 by René Lavocat

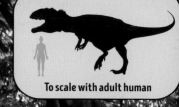

To scale with adult human

NO ESCAPE
To kill its prey, Majungasaurus relied on biting into an animal and holding on tight. This is the strategy that cats use to attack birds and mice today. Theropods—and modern dogs—snap at their prey instead. Majungasaurus's jaws clamped down on a meal rather than slashing and tearing. Once caught, there was no escape. The short, broad, tall skull of Majungasaurus and its thick, muscular neck meant it could keep its head steady while gripping a thrashing animal.

Well-preserved vertebrae with air holes show that Majungasaurus had a respiratory system like that of birds.

Its strong, muscular legs kept Majungasaurus stable when it attacked a large, heavy animal.

EAT YOUR OWN
Majungasaurus is the only dinosaur for which there is good fossil evidence of cannibalism: that it ate other animals of its own type. Majungasaurus bones have been found with tooth marks made by another Majungasaurus. However, we can't know from gnawed bones whether Majungasaurus actually killed others of its kind or whether it only ate them after they had already died.

Modern Komodo dragons sometimes kill each other when fighting for food, and the winner will eat the loser.

THE WRONG DINO

The bone of the Majungasauus crest was quite spongy, and when it was first discovered, it was mistaken for the bony dome of a pachycephalosaur. This new—but nonexistent—pachycephalosaur was named Majungatholus. This was quite exciting for dinosaur scientists at the time, as no pachycephalosaur had ever been found south of the equator. But experts soon realized it was a mistake, and there is still no known southern pachycephalosaur.

Majungasaurus renewed its teeth at least twice as quickly as other theropods —they clearly had a hard life!

Because they curved backwards, Majungasaurus teeth acted rather like fish hooks. As an animal struggled to get away, it was pulling against the curve of the teeth, driving them further into its flesh.

The four very short fingers were probably not flexible and might not even have had claws.

SEPARATE HEADS

Two bony crests and a spike on its head make Majungosaurus look different from other abelisaurs, though they also had head ornaments. Carnotaurus, in Argentina, had two horns above its eyes, and Rajasaurus, in India, had a single horn grown from its nose bone.

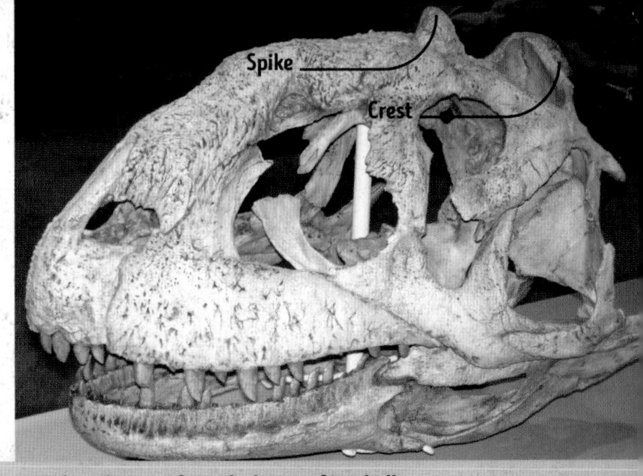

Spike

Crest

Majungasaurus's spike grew from the bones of its skull.

MASSOSPONDYLUS

Despite its sauropod-like shape, Massospondylus ran around the South African woodlands on its hind legs nearly 200 million years ago. It was a prosauropod: prosauropods were ancestors of the much larger sauropods, which spent much or all of their time on four legs.

AFRICA

FACT FILE
Name: *Massospondylus carinatus*
Lived: South Africa; 200-183 million years ago
Size: Weight 770 lb. (350 kg); length 10-13 ft. (3-4 m)
Diet: Leaves
Discovered: In 1853 by Joseph Orpen; named in 1854 by Richard Owen

To scale with adult human

DINOSAURS ON THE MOVE

Prosauropods were some of the earliest types of dinosaurs. Although Massospondylus is found only in South Africa, other prosauropod fossils have been found elsewhere. It seems that the prosauropods spread around the world when all the land was connected in a single supercontinent. When the land split up, they evolved differently in different areas. How they evolved partly depended on the food available and the predators that wanted to eat them.

Massospondylus lived where it was quite hot and dry. This might often have limited its size, as plants don't grow well in dry areas. The dinosaur could keep growing if there was plenty of food.

INSIDE THE EGG

A clutch of fossilized Massospondylus eggs has revealed how the embryos developed in their eggs. More than 40 years after they were found, scientists have the technology to scan them with powerful microscopes and build computer models of the bones. The curled-up embryos are 6 in. (15 cm) long and were just over halfway through their time in the egg. Their legs are all the same length, suggesting the hatchlings may have run around on four feet.

Scientists have scanned the skull of a fossilized embryo, such as this, and found tiny teeth in the jaws less than ¼ in. (0.5 mm) across.

DOWN IN ONE

Massospondylus might have been an omnivore, eating plants and small animals, such as lizards or dinosaur hatchlings. Its teeth were not good for chewing, so it would have swallowed tougher plant matter straight down. It had small stones embedded in its stomach lining that helped to mash up the leaves once the dinosaur had swallowed them.

Theropod-like teeth for eating meat were at the front of the mouth.

Massonspondylus had two types of teeth. Some were adapted to eating plants, but others could have coped with meat.

The long neck and small head were shared with later sauropods, but the body and legs were very different.

Prosauropods that stood on two legs, like Massospondylus, probably used the large claws on their fingers when gathering food.

Like some other dinosaurs, Massospondylus probably carried on growing throughout its life.

NEST SITES

Massospondylus's nest sites have up to 10 nests each, suggesting herd or group living. Each nest had up to 34 eggs, each about 2 in. (6 cm) long, and with shells just ¼ in. (0.2–0.3 mm) thick. Animals in danger from predators often lay large numbers of eggs to make sure that at least some young survive and grow to adulthood. The hatchlings might have stayed in the nest until they doubled their size.

Today, sea turtles lay around 100 eggs at a time, but not many of the young hatchlings survive.

NIGERSAURUS

Sometimes called a Cretaceous lawn mower, Nigersaurus had a wide jaw that it held close to the ground to graze on low-growing plants. It was probably a common sight on the wooded floodplains of Cretaceous Niger, in much the same way that grazing antelope are plentiful in modern Niger.

AFRICA

FACT FILE
Name: *Nigersaurus taqueti*
Lived: Niger, Nigeria; 115-105 million years ago
Size: Weight 8,800 lb. (4,000 kg); length 29 ft. (9 m)
Diet: Low-growing ferns, shrubs, and flowering plants
Discovered: In 1965-1972 by Philippe Taquet; named in 1999 by Paul Sereno

To scale with adult human

EXTRAORDINARY JAW

In many ways, Nigersaurus was an unremarkable, medium-sized sauropod, but its jaw sets it apart, not only from other sauropods or even other dinosaurs, but all other four-legged animals. Its jaw was broader at the front than the rest of its skull, a shape not found in any other animal.

Very few fossils of Nigersaurus have been found because its bones were so thin and hollow they didn't preserve well. Parts of its backbone and skull were so thin that light could shine through them!

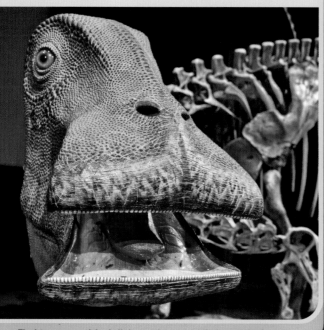

The bizarre mouth had all the teeth in a straight line at the front.

STRAIGHT NOT CURVED

Most animals have a row of teeth that follows the curve of the jaw (as yours do), but Nigersaurus had a single straight row of teeth, top and bottom. The teeth in the top jaw were probably slightly smaller than those in the lower jaw. Each tooth was long and curved, but not especially sharp. They wore out quickly—each lasted only 14 days before being shed and replaced.

It may have had a covering of keratin, like a beak, at the sides of its jaw.

THIN AND HOLLOW

Apart from the legs, much of Nigersaurus's skeleton was made of thin, hollow bones with large air spaces inside. Its skull had large openings, or fenestrae, like those of other dinosaurs, but the holes were especially big in Nigersaurus. Because of this, only ½ sq. in. (1 sq cm) of bone connected the back of the head to the snout and was only ¼ in. (2 mm) thick!

The Nigersaurus jaw held around 500 teeth arranged in closely packed rows. Each row had nine reserve teeth ready to replace the tooth in use.

NOSE TO THE GROUND

With front legs only two-thirds the length of the back legs, Nigersaurus slanted downward to the front. It had a short neck (for a sauropod) that could probably not stretch upward, so its head was generally pointing toward the ground. Experts think Nigersaurus usually kept its head low, cropping short, soft plants. It couldn't open its mouth very wide, so fed in the same way as a cow grazing on grass.

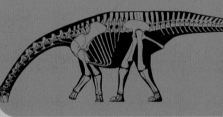

Scientists don't agree about whether Nigersaurus always kept its head low, or only dipped it to eat and otherwise had the same horizontal posture as other sauropods.

The limbs of Nigersaurus were sturdy and robust, like those of other sauropods, despite many of the other bones being light and thin.

OURANOSAURUS

Ouranosaurus was a close relative of the hadrosaurs. Its most noticeable features was a hump or sail on its back. This was supported by bony growths from its backbone, called neural spines.

AFRICA

FACT FILE
Name: *Ouranosaurus nigeriensis*
Lived: Niger; 125-100 million years ago
Size: Weight 4,850-8,800 lb. (2,200-4,000 kg); length 26 ft. (8 m)
Diet: Soft plants, perhaps fruit and seeds
Discovered: In 1965 by Philippe Taquet; named in 1976 by Philippe Taquet

To scale with adult human

SAIL AWAY

Many dinosaurs had neural spines. On some other sauropods, they made a row of short spikes along the back. The spines from Ouranosaurus's back were too long just to stick out of the surface, though, and had broad, flat ends. They must have been covered with flesh in some form. They might have been the framework for a hump, or a thick and fleshy sail.

Ouranosaurus's nostrils were high on its snout, suggesting that it fed at ground level. Nostrils at the end of the snout could easily become blocked with dirt, so having them on top prevented that.

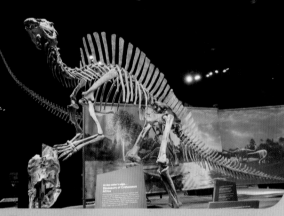

The long neural spines ran from the base of the neck to the tail.

An extra inflexible finger at the side of its forefoot meant Ouranosaurus could spread its weight when it was standing on all fours. This would help it to avoid sinking into muddy ground.

HUMP LUMP

A sail might have helped with temperature control, or perhaps made a display to attract a mate or show other Ouranosaurus this animal was one of them. Alternatively, if the spines supported a hump, this might have given the dinosaur a way of storing food energy, as a camel does today. A camel eats when food is plentiful, building up fat in its hump. It can break this down and use the energy from it when there is a shortage of food.

Like camels, perhaps Ouranosaurus stored fat in a hump.

LOW LIFE

Ouranosaurus lived in low-lying areas, such as the places where rivers flow into the sea, and where there are not many trees. The ground would have been muddy, and Ouranosaurus probably fed on low-growing plants. It had a thumb spike like Iguanodon, but not the flexible fifth finger that Iguanodon used to grip plants. Iguanodon used this while standing on its hind legs to hold plants it was pulling on to eat, but Ouranosaurus had no need for it.

Ouranosaurus fed right from the ground, so it didn't need to hold its food as this Iguanodon did .

The neural spines were largest behind the shoulders, where they were 25 in. (63 cm) long.

It probably did not run fast, as a fairly short tail with weak muscles offered little support for balance while running.

BEAKY AND GAPPY

Ouranosaurus had a mouth well adapted to pulling up the soft plants that grow at the water's edge. After a gap behind the beak, it had 88 small teeth arranged in rows. Each fully functional tooth was followed by one that was just emerging, ready to replace it. These teeth might have helped Ouranosaurus to bite through firmer plant stems, or mash up leaves a little, so that they could be digested more quickly.

The jaw muscles were not strong, so Ouranosaurus could not have eaten tough plant matter.

SARCOSUCHUS

The Sahara Desert in northern Africa is now parched land, but a hundred million years ago, it was filled with lush vegetation and many rivers. Sarcosuchus lived in the rivers and swamps of this tropical wetland but was not a dinosaur. It was a crocodyliforme—a crocodile-shaped animal of a type called a pholidosaur.

AFRICA

FACT FILE
Name: *Sarcosuchus imperator*
Lived: Algeria, Tunisia, Morocco, Niger, possibly Libya; 129-112 million years ago;
Size: Weight 7,700 lb. (3,500 kg); length 31 ft. (9.5 m)
Diet: Fish, possibly dinosaurs
Discovered: In 1946-59 by Albert-Félix de Lapparent; named in 1966 by France de Broin and Phillipe Taquet

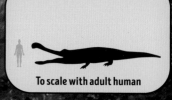
To scale with adult human

HARD SKIN
Modern crocodiles have bony scales growing in their skin, and Sarcosuchus had these, too. Called osteoderms or scutes, they gave it an armored outside. Modern crocodiles have gaps between scutes, but Sarcosuchus was fully covered over nearly all its body.

Sarcosuchus had a short but powerful tail that meant it could swim fast to chase fish.

The length of Sarcosuchus has been calculated from the width of its skull and the length of the femur (thigh bone). Sarcosuchus could probably reach nearly 33 ft. (10 m)—and it kept growing throughout its life.

GONE FISHING
While a large Sarcosuchus could have been an ambush predator, waiting in the water to seize dinosaurs that came to drink, it probably ate fish most of the time. Its style of jaw is better suited to snapping fish than wrestling with a large land animal. Young Sarcosuchus had a narrow snout. Only when the animal was older and very large did the snout grow wider. Perhaps it ate fish until this stage and then started snatching animals from the shore.

Sarcosuchus could have eaten giant prehistoric fish such as this Mawsonia, which grew up to 18 ft. (6 m) long.

BOBBLY NOSE

The strange-looking blob on the end of Sarcosuchus's snout is called a bulla. No one is quite sure what it was for. It might have been to attract a mate—maybe males with a large bulla were more likely to find a female partner. It could perhaps have been used for butting against rival males in tussles for territory or mates.

The bulla might have held some special organ of smell, or provided a way of making or amplifying noises.

MEASURING THE MISSING

As with many other extinct animals, no complete skeleton of Sarcosuchus has been found. When parts are missing, it's hard to judge how large the animal would have been. Paleontologists often figure out the size of incomplete prehistoric animals by comparing the size of bones they do have to equivalent bones in similar animals of a known size.

Fossil bones are carefully wrapped before being taken away for examination. This is called jacketing.

Because it was covered in hard bony scales, Sarcosuchus had a body that was quite stiff everywhere except for the tip of the tail and the top of the head.

One of the largest crocodyliformes there has ever been, Sarcosuchus is nicknamed "supercroc."

Because of the structure of the bones in its head, Sarcosuchus's eyes could swivel up and down but not left to right.

Its teeth and jaws were well adapted to fish-eating. The top jaw hooked over the lower jaw slightly so it could grip slippery prey.

The long snout took up three-quarters of the length of the skull and held 132 teeth.

SPINOSAURUS

Spinosaurus is not only the largest meat-eating dinosaur yet discovered, it was also the first swimming dinosaur to be found. Several of its features make it clear that Spinosaurus lived largely in the water.

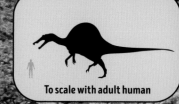

To scale with adult human

FACT FILE
Name: *Spinosaurus aegyptiacus*
Lived: Egypt, Morocco; 112-97 million years ago
Size: Weight 14,000-16,500 lb. (6,400-7,500 kg); length 52 ft. (16 m)
Diet: Fish, possibly reptiles
Discovered: In 1912 by Ernst Stromer von Reichenbach; named in 1915 by Ernst Stromer von Reichenbach

SHORT LEGS

Most theropods had a large pelvis (hip area) and long, powerful legs for running quickly on land, but Spinosaurus had short back legs and its pelvis was small. It might have walked on all four legs at least some of the time—which was rare for a theropod—and wasn't well suited to running fast after prey. Instead, it hunted in the water.

Spinosaurus had straight claws on its foot, unlike many other theropods.

The vertebrae in its tail were connected more loosely than in the tails of other theropods, making Spinosaurus very flexible. This means it could use its tail like a paddle to help propel it through the water.

We can't tell from fossils whether Spinosaurus had webbed feet, but webs could have helped it swim and walk on muddy ground.

TOP NOSTRILS

To help it breathe with its mouth in the water, Spinosaurus nostrils were on top of its snout. Its wide feet and flat claws could spread its weight and keep it steady on a muddy riverbed. Its long body and neck would have made the front end quite heavy. That would have been a disadvantage on land, making it unstable on its hind legs, but could have helped it move in water.

Like crocodiles today, Spinosaurus might have waited at the water's surface for fish to pass by.

FISH DINNERS

It's clear from its mouth and teeth that Spinosaurus ate fish. Like the teeth of fish-eating plesiosaurs and pterosaurs, these were snaggly and well-spaced, perfect for snapping slippery fish. Spinosaurus could tackle large fish, including small sharks. It had a mix of large and small teeth, but none had serrated edges like the teeth of land-going theropods for slicing through the tough flesh of other reptiles.

This reconstruction shows what a Spinosaurus might have looked like hunting underwater.

Supported by neural spines, the Spinosaurus sail was just over 6 ft. (2 m) tall at its highest point.

Its long, narrow snout, nearly 6 ft. (2 m) long, was packed with short but sharp teeth.

SAILING IN THE RIVER

Its gigantic sail was another way in which Spinosaurus differed from other theropods. Skin stretched between the spines was probably boldly colored and could have been used to attract a mate or to signal to other Spinosaurus. The bones of the spine were connected with ball-and-socket-type joints (like the ones you have in your shoulders), which meant the dinosaur could possibly have arched its back to spread out its sail more visibly when it wanted to.

With its sail spread, Spinosaurus would have been a scary sight.

SUCHOMIMUS

In many ways, Suchomimus looks like a small Spinosaurus (pp.122-23) with less of a sail. It also looks a bit like a large Baryonyx (pp.76-77), but with a sail. Its similarity to Baryonyx is puzzling, as Africa and the islands of Europe had been separated by the Tethys Sea for a long time when Suchomimus lived.

AFRICA

FACT FILE
Name: *Suchomimus tenerensis*
Lived: Niger; 125-112 million years ago
Size: Weight 5,500-11,500 lb. (2,500-5,200 kg); length 31-36 ft. (9.5-11 m)
Diet: Fish, pterosaurs, and small dinosaurs
Discovered: In 1997 by David Varricchio; named in 1998 by Paul Sereno

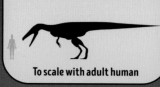
To scale with adult human

TWO OR ONE?

Some paleontologists believe that Suchomimus and Baryonyx are different dinosaurs. Others suggest that they are the same dinosaur at different ages and stages of development. Baryonyx is known only from fossils of young animals, and Suchomimus from an individual that was nearly adult. If the neural spines and the sail they support didn't begin to grow until the animal began to mature, Baryonyx might be a young animal with no sail, and Suchomimus might be the same type of animal once its sail had begun to grow in.

It's easy to see how Baryonyx might grow up to be Suchomimus. The surviving bones of both are very similar shapes; those of Suchomimus are just larger.

Neural spines supported a tail sail on the dinosaur's back. They were tallest over the hips and carried on to the mid-tail.

BIG FISH

Suchomimus (and Spinosaurus) lived alongside many other creatures, including other theropods, hadrosaurs, sauropods, crocodyliformes, pterosaurs, and also early mammals, birds, and arthropods, such as insects. Spinosaurs like Suchomimus avoided competing with large, faster theropods that hunted prey on land by eating fish and other animals from the rivers and by picking up carrion. They avoided competing for fish with pterosaurs by being much larger, so they would eat fish that were far too big for a pterosaur to catch.

The backward curving teeth were adapted to holding on to slippery, struggling fish.

BETTER HUNTER

Hunting big fish meant that Spinosaurs were competing with crocodyliformes, including Sarcosuchus. Here, they had advantages of speed, flexibility, height, and hands. Crocodiles generally lie in shallow water and wait for prey. Spinosaurs could swim around, or (like Suchomimus) stand in the shallows looking down into the water. They were also better at hunting extra food on land than crocodiles.

Suchomimus had more teeth than a Spinosaurus, and they were larger at the front. Spinosaurus had straight teeth, while Suchomimus had curved, serrated teeth.

Spinosaurs, including Suchomimus, had a huge slashing claw on each front hand, which they could use against small or medium-sized dinosaurs.

Its giant claw was the first part of Suchomimus to be found.

Suchomimus's feet have never been found, but it's likely they were similar to the feet of other spinosaurid dinosaurs, with large, curved claws on three toes.

PICKY EATER

Suchomimus lived in the warm, wet floodplains of the land that is now Niger. This was a lush landscape, rich in different species of animals, as rainforests are today. When a lot of animals live together in a small space, many become quite specialized in their feeding habits, so that they don't have to compete with so many other animals when hunting for food.

Like Suchomimus, koalas specialize in one type of food. They live in the forests of Australia, where they eat only the leaves of eucalyptus trees.

ASIA

Many dinosaur fossils have been found in Asia, but most in just a few places. Exposed rock of the right age to hold dinosaur fossils is most common in China and Mongolia, but there are also dinosaurs from Thailand, India, Korea, Japan, and Russia. By 2006, more than 200 different types of dinosaurs had been found at over 100 sites in Asia, and many more have emerged since.

PSITTACOSAURUS (pp.150–51)
Mongolia

CITIPATI (pp.130–31)
Mongolia

THERIZINOSAURUS (pp.156–57)
Mongolia

CAUDIPTERYX (pp.128–29)
China

VELOCIRAPTOR (pp.158–59)
Mongolia

MICRORAPTOR (pp.144–45)
China

HUAYANGOSAURUS (pp.138–39)
China

MONOLOPHOSAURUS (pp.146–47)
China

DINOSAURS ON THE MOVE

As the supercontinent Pangaea split up, North America remained joined to Asia for a long time. Animals could cross a land bridge at Alaska, moving between areas that would later be separated. Even when the lands did part, similar climates and landscapes in both regions led many dinosaurs to evolve in similar ways, as we can see from their fossils. Where North America has Tyrannosaurus rex (pp.46–47), Asia has Tarbosaurus (pp.154–55). Where America has Stegosaurus (pp.42–43), Asia has a number of different stegosaurs. And where America has Triceratops (pp.43), Asia has its own varieties of ceratopsians.

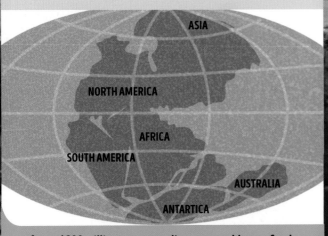

Around 200 million years ago, dinosaurs could move freely around the connected lands of the northern hemisphere. The lands did not separate until around 170 million years ago.

DRAGONS OF THE EAST

Chinese legends about animals such as dragons and griffons might have started when dinosaur fossils were found thousands of years ago. Earlier societies often thought the fossilized bones they found had special powers, and sometimes included these "dragon bones" in medicinal mixtures.

OVERHEAD AND UNDERFOOT

The first early mammal fossils were found in China and date from more than 150 million years ago. These little animals, many of which looked rather like shrews, lived in trees and burrows, out of the way of the large feet and teeth of dinosaurs. Quite a few were probably nocturnal, coming out when dinosaurs might have been sleeping. After the dinosaurs were gone, they would diversify into all the mammals we have now—from whales and tigers to mice, camels, and humans.

EGGS AND BONES

The flaming cliffs at Bayanzag in Mongolia (shown here) are in the Gobi desert. The desert is freezing in winter and hot for a brief summer. The extreme weather helps to expose fossils, blowing away sand and eroding rock. Many dinosaur fossils have been found here, including clutches of eggs. As the land was desert even in the Cretaceous, many dinosaur bones have remained undisturbed where they fell, 70 million years ago.

Early mammals like Juramaia were all small, and many probably made a snack for dinosaurs. Juramaia lived in China 160 million years ago.

CAUDIPTERYX

The bird-like Caudipteryx was less than 3 ft. (1 m) long. It had a boxy head and long legs well adapted to running fast, as well as a cluster of long feathers on its tail and wings. All Caudipteryx fossils that have been discovered were found in a single area in China that was once a prehistoric lake.

ASIA

FACT FILE
Name: *Caudipteryx zoui*
Lived: Liaoning Province (China); 120-130 million years ago
Size: Weight 5 lb. (2.2 kg); length 32 in. (80 cm)
Diet: Omnivorous: plants and meat
Discovered: In 1997 by Ji Qiang; named in 1998 by Ji Qiang

To scale with adult human

FEATHERED ARMS

The whole of Caudipteryx's body was covered with downy feathers, but its arms had at least one row of much longer feathers. These were as long as the flight feathers of some birds, although Caudipteryx couldn't fly. Its arms were too short to be wings, and even its longer feathers were too short for flight. Its feathers kept it warm and might have been used in display.

The fan on the tail might have been used to attract a mate.

As a small, flightless animal in a region full of predators, Caudipteryx probably needed to run for its life quite a lot!

A BEAK PLUS

Caudipteryx had a beak, although it was slightly different from that of a modern bird in that it had teeth. These were deeply rooted in its jaw and were long and sharp, suggesting the animal ate meat. It was probably an omnivore, eating both meat and some plant material, such as seeds, fruit, and leaves.

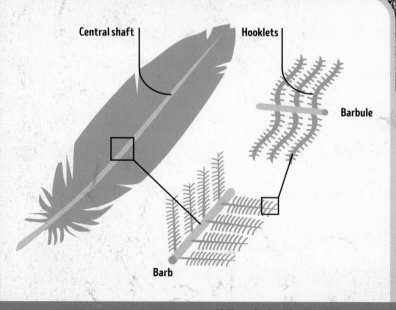

Central shaft

Hooklets

Barbule

Barb

FEATHERS, FILAMENTS, AND FLUFF

The outer layer of feathers on modern birds has a central shaft with lots of barbs coming off it on either side. These have rows of barbules, which are "zipped" together by tiny hooks. The barbules and hooks interlock and hold the feather in shape and put it back together if it gets ruffled. This type of feather is called a pennaceous feather. Caudipteryx had these "proper" feathers. Some other dinosaurs had feathers that could trap air and keep them warm, but were not sleek and did not define the animal's shape like pennaceous feathers.

Modern-day bird feathers are made up of several parts that all work together.

BIRD BONES

Caudipteryx had light bones very like those of modern birds. It even had a wishbone as modern-day birds do—a forked bone that acts as a strut between the shoulders.

Its long legs were used to run after prey or to wade into water to hunt for fish.

BIRD AND BACK

It seems strange that birds would evolve from flightless dinosaurs to being able to fly, and then for some species to evolve back to being flightless. But several modern birds have done this, including penguins, which swim instead, ostriches, which run, and ground-living birds, such as the kakapo from New Zealand.

The flightless kakapo is now endangered.

The wing feathers might have helped the dinosaur to steer when running fast.

BIRD OR DINOSAUR?

Caudipteryx is one of many types of feathered dinosaurs discovered in Asia in the last 30 years. Most feathered dinosaurs—including Caudipteryx—could not fly, but modern birds have evolved from some of them. A link between birds and dinosaurs was first suggested by an English biologist, Thomas Henry Huxley, in 1869, but for a long time people thought the idea was ridiculous. It became more popular in the 1980s, and the discovery of Caudipteryx and two other feathered dinosaurs, Sinosauropteryx and Protarchaeopteryx, finally persuaded many experts that the link is real.

CITIPATI

Nearly as tall as an adult human, Citipati ran around the Mongolian desert 70 million years ago. It looked something like a giant turkey, with a small head and neck but a large body. It had long, powerful legs for speed, topped off with a short, feathered tail.

ASIA

FACT FILE
Name: *Citipati osmolskae*
Lived: Mongolia; 75-71 million years ago
Size: Weight 165-180 lb. (75-88 kg); length 10 ft. (3 m)
Diet: Plants, small animals, and perhaps eggs
Discovered: In 1993; named in 2001 by Rinchen Barsbold, James Clark, and Mark Norel

To scale with adult human

BIG BIRD
Citipati was one of the largest oviraptors (pp. 148–49)—a type of two-legged, large-brained dinosaur that cared for its eggs. Though not a bird, Citipati had many bird-like features. Its jaw had hardened into a beak with no teeth, and it was strong like a parrot's.

Like modern ostriches, Cititpati probably ran around the desert snapping up insects and small reptiles as well as munching on plants.

Citipati had a short tail, with a clutch of long feathers fanning out at the end.

Citipati's body was probably covered with feathers. These would have helped to insulate the eggs it sat on.

ON THE NEST
One of the most remarkable fossils we have is of a Citipati adult sitting on top of eggs. The eggs are arranged in layers in a circular nest on a mound of earth. Citipati has been nicknamed "Big Mama" and could sit on 22 eggs at a time. It sat on its nest with its arms stretched out, as modern flightless birds, such as ostriches, do. This would keep the eggs warm, or shade them from the hot sun.

This model egg shows what an unhatched Citipati embryo looked like.

AIR HEAD

Citipati's head is topped off with a low crest, rather like the crest of some modern birds, such as the cassowary. It was made from an extension of the bones of the skull. Like the cassowary, Citipati may have used it to protect its head as it ran through vegetation or to amplify the sounds it made.

The cassowary's crest is hard on the outside but has a honeycomb of air spaces inside.

Citipati's skull has been so well preserved that scientists have been able to scan the inside and figure out the structure of its brain.

The bones of Citipati's skull are riddled with air holes, which make the skull light.

Citipati supported its weight on three clawed toes, well adapted to running over dry land.

TWO BY TWO

Citipati laid their eggs in pairs, neatly arranged in the nest. This tells experts that Citipati had two working oviducts, or tubes, for delivering eggs. Modern birds have only one oviduct and lay their eggs in jumbled clusters. A mother Citipati probably laid pairs of eggs repeatedly over several days and sat on them when she had laid enough.

Citipati eggs were long, narrow, and neatly laid out.

DEINOCHEIRUS

The story of Deinocheirus is one of the strangest in the history of dinosaur discovery. It began in 1965, when a pair of giant hands and arms with attached shoulder blades, but no other body parts, were found in the desert of Mongolia.

FACT FILE
Name: *Deinocheirus mirificus*
Lived: Mongolia; 70 million years ago
Size: Weight 14,100-15,500 lb. (6,400-7,000 kg); length 39 ft. (12 m)
Diet: Plants, carrion, small animals, insects, fish
Discovered: In 1965 by Zofia Kielan-Jaworowska; named in 1970 by Halszka Osmólska and Ewa Roniewicz

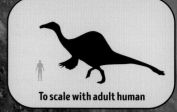
To scale with adult human

TERRIBLE HANDS

The powerful, muscular arms, at 8 ft. (2.5 m) long, suggested a huge animal. The three-fingered hands, with immense curved claws, suggested a savage one. Investigation showed that it was a theropod, but these often have small arms. Deinocheirus remained a mystery for nearly 50 years, until more fossils were discovered in 2013, making a nearly complete skeleton.

A sail or hump on the back was supported by neural spines—bony spurs growing from the vertebrae.

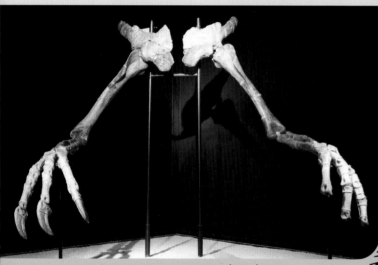
The curved claws are up to 8 in. (20 cm) long.

HOOK AND PULL

The claws, instead of slashing or gripping flesh, appear to have been used to hook onto and pull the stems or branches of plants or to dig up roots, but the hands could not flex enough to grasp well. The similarity between the claws of the plant-eating sloth and those of Deinocheirus show that long, curved claws don't have to be used for hunting.

The three-toed sloth uses its long claws to climb and hang from trees.

Its long, narrow skull was nearly 3 ft. (1 m) long but only 9 in. (23 cm) across at its widest point.

Calculating the animal's size from its large arms at first led paleontologists to believe Deinocheirus was even larger than it really was.

Bird-like beaked dinosaurs usually had quite a large brain, but Deinocheirus had an exceptionally small brain.

GIANT SCAVENGER

Despite its fearsome-looking claws, Deinocheirus was not a hunter. It was an omnivore, and probably ate plants much of the time. It also scavenged for carrion and would eat any small animal that came its way. One fossil has been found with fish scales that seem to be the remains of its last meal. Fish might have been a major part of Deinocheirus's diet, as its toothless, horny beak has a spoon-shaped end, like that of some modern fish-eating birds.

The spoonbill uses its beak to scoop up fish, and Deinocheirus might have done the same.

DILONG

Surprisingly, Dilong was an early type of tyrannosaur, though far smaller than the later terrifying tyrannosaur predators. It was the first tyrannosaur known to have feathers. The discovery raised the possibility that more tyrannosaurs might have had feathers —perhaps even T. rex (pp.46-47), at least when very young.

ASIA

FACT FILE

Name: *Dilong paradoxus*
Lived: Liaoning (China); 125 million years ago
Size: Weight 35 lb. (16 kg); length 6 ft. (2 m)
Diet: Small dinosaurs, lizards, mammals, birds
Discovered: In 2004 by Xu Xing; named in 2004 by Xu Xing

To scale with adult human

KEEPING WARM

Dilong fossils show that its body was entirely covered with feathers. These were not the same types of feathers as modern birds have, but were simple "protofeathers" more like bristles. Dilong did not fly, so these basic feathers were used to keep the animal warm.

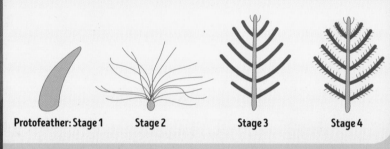

Protofeather: Stage 1   Stage 2   Stage 3   Stage 4

Feathers evolved from the simplest of protofeathers to modern bird feathers.

Dilong's arms were longer for its body size than the arms of later tyrannosaurs.

DON'T RUSH!

When fossils are found in large slabs of rock, they can be removed for experts to work on elsewhere. But when fossils are lodged in crumbly rock or sand, as Dilong was, all the work to remove them has to be done in the field.

Slow and careful work with a paintbrush is needed to uncover fossils without damaging them.

Unlike other tyrannosaurs, Dilong had a bony Y-shaped crest on its skull, with ridges running down either side of its snout.

CHINESE STYLE

The name Dilong means "emperor dragon" in Chinese. While dinosaur names often end with "saurus," meaning "lizard" in Greek, Chinese dinosaurs names often end with "long," meaning "dragon."

NOT THE USUAL TYRANNOSAUR

As well as being small, Dilong was an unusual tyrannosaur in other ways. It had long thighs, but the lower part of its rear legs was shorter (for its size) than in later tyrannosaurs, so it could probably not run as fast. It was still fast enough to hunt its prey in the forested floodplains and volcanic lowlands.

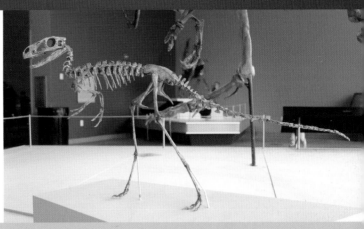

Dilong's arms were long enough to hold on to its prey, unlike T. rex's.

Dilong had three large toes that rested on the ground and a dewclaw—a tiny, extra toe that came out further up the foot and never touched the ground.

UNDER THE VOLCANO

Fossils of Dilong come from an area of China that had volcanoes 130 million years ago. Many fossils from the region are very well preserved because the animals were gently covered with falling volcanic ash. This means they were not crushed or destroyed by scavengers and did not rot away before beginning to fossilize.

This fossil of Dilong shows the neck curved around , so that the head lies over the back.

FAT OR FEATHERS?

To stay warm, an animal can grow a layer of fat or blubber, or cover its outside with feathers or fur. Growing fat or blubber makes the animal heavier and often slower. For an active hunter, feathers are light and effective.

A walrus has a thick layer of fat to keep it warm but is slow and awkward on land.

On each hand Dilong had three fingers. Other tyrannosaurs had two fingers.

GALLIMIMUS

The largest of the ostrich-like dinosaurs called ornithomimids, Gallimimus ran around the plains of Mongolia 70 million years ago on its long legs. Although its running style and long neck were like those of an ostrich, the long, thick tail made the animal very different from modern running birds.

ASIA

FACT FILE

Name: *Gallimimus*
Lived: Mongolia; 70 million years ago
Size: Weight 260 lb. (120 kg); length 18-26 ft. (5.5-8 m)
Diet: Possibly insects, small mammals, fruit
Discovered: In 1963 by Zofia Kielan-Jaworowska; named in 1972 by Halszka Osmólska, Rinchen Barsbold, and Ewa Roniewicz

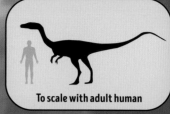

To scale with adult human

A WET WORLD

The part of Mongolia where Gallimimus lived was probably wet, with river channels, streams, lakes, and mudflats. This would have offered it a variety of food but would also have been good hunting ground for large theropods such as Tarbosaurus (pp.154–55), which would have been a threat to Gallimimus. Its speed would have been Gallimimus's main defense against being eaten.

GROUP OUTING

A Gallimimus foot and trackway found in 2009 set a puzzle for paleontologists. The foot was preserved in mudstone and the tracks in sandstone, and it was 8 in. (20 cm) lower than the tracks. The foot probably didn't make the tracks, but the pair together suggest that many Gallimimus had been in the area over some time. Empty spaces where fossils have been removed suggest a group of Gallimimus died together, and so quite possibly also lived together.

The top and bottom of the beak did not quite meet when it was closed.

Gallimimus would have used its long tail to balance while running.

The arms ended in three fingers with strong, curved claws.

With its long rear legs, Gallimimus could probably reach a top speed of about 30 mph (50 km/h). The length of the lower part of the legs meant it could cover a lot of ground with each step.

136

A BEAK LIKE A BIRD

Unlike some other ornithomimids, Gallimimus had a long head with a toothless beak. The beak was long and U-shaped at the end, rather like the beak of a modern duck. The lack of teeth makes it harder to tell what Gallimimus ate. It was possibly an omnivore, eating insects, perhaps snatching up small animals that it could swallow whole, finding seeds and fruit, and also cropping low-growing plants. It might even have eaten the eggs of other animals.

With eyes on either side of its head, the dinosaur was adapted to keeping a lookout for predators rather than hunting its own prey.

The front limbs were shorter than those of other ornithomimids. Little bumps on the bone of the lower arm, called quill knobs, show where wing feathers attached —but Gallimimus could not fly.

Although unrelated to Gallimimus (top), a modern duck has a similarly shaped beak.

Like other bird-like dinosaurs, but differing from other theropods, Gallimimus had only three toes and no dewclaw.

SMUGGLED!

The smuggling (illegal movement) of dinosaur fossils is a real problem. Countries such as Mongolia, which have only recently begun to excavate and preserve their dinosaur fossils, have had foreign hunters stealing fossils to sell abroad. Gallimimus has been a victim of this. When smuggled fossils are discovered by the authorities, they are returned to the nation from which they were stolen.

This Gallimimus fossil was one of many recovered in the USA and returned to Mongolia in 2013.

HUAYANGOSAURUS

Stegosaurs of different types have been found around the world, and one of the oldest is Huayangosaurus. It lived several million years before any other stegosaur that has yet been found, suggesting that the stegosaurs started off in the region that is now China.

FACT FILE

Name: *Huayangosaurus taibaii*
Lived: Sichuan Province (China); 168-161 million years ago
Size: Weight 1,875 lb. (850 kg); length 15 ft. (4.5 m)
Diet: Plants
Discovered: In 1979; named in 1982 by Dong Zhiming, Tang Zilu, and Zhou Shiwu

To scale with adult human

Huayangosaurus was one of the spikiest stegosaurs, with spikes on its shoulders, down its back, and on its thagomizer.

STEGOSAURS GET GOING

Differences between Huayangosaurus and later stegosaurs have helped paleontologists to figure out how the animals evolved. For example, Huayangosaurus had teeth at the front of its mouth, but later stegosaurs had a toothless beak at the front and had teeth only toward the back of the mouth. The snout was broader than in later animals, too, suggesting that it was not adapted to picking out the plants it wanted, but took mouthfuls of whatever it could grab.

It had seven teeth at the top front of its mouth on each side.

PLATE STATE

The plates on the back of Huayangosaurus were more spikelike and thicker than those of many later stegosaurs. Stegosaurus's (pp.40–41) larger plates would not have been good for defense because they were too thin and fragile. Their large area would have helped if Stegosaurus used them to control its temperature. Huayangosaurus had plates better suited to defense but of little use for temperature control.

Its strong, spiky plates would have been great protection against attack by predators.

WALKING THE WORLD

Several different kinds of stegosaurs have been found in China, but they are also found on all other continents except Antarctica. Early stegosaurs probably emerged in China and spread from there to the rest of the world. When the lands finally separated, the isolated stegosaurs evolved separately —still recognizably related, but with different features that suited the environment in which each type lived.

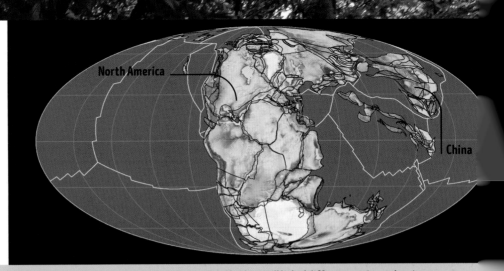

North America

China

The world's landmasses were breaking up when Huayangosaurus was alive, but land bridges still linked different continental regions.

Huayangosaurus had a partially stiffened tail, which it could swing like a club at enemies.

PLATES AND SPIKES

The wider skull of Huayangosaurus is similar to the skull shape of ankylosaurs. Another skull, 50 million years older than Huayangosaurus, was once identified as an ankylosaur but later turned out to be closer to Huayangosaurus. It's possible that Huayangosaurus was an early descendant of an animal that led to both ankylosaurs and stegosaurs.

Huayangosaurus was smaller than many later stegosaurs and around half the length of Stegosaurus.

Huayangosaurus had a wider and shorter head shape than Stegosaurus's banana-shaped head.

HUPEHSUCHUS

The fish-shaped Hupehsuchus was a marine reptile that lived near the shores of Triassic China. It looks similar to Ichthyosaurus (pp.84-85) but they are not directly related. They might have shared a common ancestor, or might have evolved in similar ways because they had similar lifestyles.

FACT FILE

Name: *Hupehsuchus nanchangensis*

Lived: Hubei Province (China); 242 million years ago

Size: Length 39 in. (100 cm)

Diet: Unknown

Discovered: Named in 1972 by Yang Zhongjian and Dong Zhiming

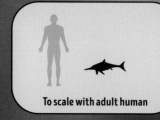

To scale with adult human

WELL ARMORED

Hupehsuchus had rows of bony plates on its back and belly. Experts don't think Hupehsuchus needed this armor for protection, as it probably had few predators. Perhaps it developed the plates before it adapted to living in water— they might have protected its ancestors on land.

Its plates made Hupehsuchus less flexible, but they were reduced toward the tail end, so the tail could flex from side to side.

EATING WITH ITS MOUTH OPEN

No one knows exactly what Hupehsuchus ate or how it ate it. One possibility is that it sifted food out of the water, perhaps with some kind of filter in its mouth that hasn't fossilized. If so, it probably had its mouth open when keeping still in the water or swimming slowly to catch fish. Alternatively, it might have snapped up small animals it could swallow whole.

Hupehsuchus may have feasted on squid and other marine invertebrates.

TRIASSIC ODDITY

Hupehsuchus had an odd mixture of features. Its fossil has a tiny skull with a very long, narrow snout that looks a little like a bird's skull and beak. The snout is like that of Ichthyosaurus, but Hupehsuchus had no teeth, while Ichthyosaurus's jaws were packed with teeth.

Its body looks rather squashed front to back, making Hupehsuchus short and stocky.

Rows of bony plates formed a line of armor along Hupehsuchus's back, and made the top of it quite heavy.

HIDDEN FINGERS AND TOES

Hupehsuchus had seven fingers on each "hand" and six toes on each "foot." However, the front limbs were fused into flippers and the back limbs into paddles, so the bones were all lined up inside and didn't make separate external fingers and toes.

Some species of Hupehsuchus had belly ribs—extra bones that supported and protected the animal's wide belly.

MAMENCHISAURUS

A fossil found on a Chinese construction site in the 1950s turned out to have one of the longest necks of all sauropods, with more neck vertebrae than any other dinosaur. Mamenchisaurus was not the largest sauropod, but its neck was longer than that of much larger animals.

FACT FILE

Name: *Mamenchisaurus constructus*
Lived: Sichuan (China), Mongolia; 160-145 million years ago
Size: Length 49 ft. (15 m)
Diet: Plants
Discovered: In 1952; named in 1954 by Yang Zhongjian

To scale with adult human

NECK OF THE WOODS?

It's not clear why Mamenchisaurus needed such a long neck. One suggestion is that a long neck enabled it to reach into woodland areas where its body couldn't fit, in order to feed on plants there. It might also have been able to pluck plants from boggy ground at a bit of a distance, so that its bulk didn't sink into the soft soil.

Mamenchisaurus's extra-long neck meant its head could reach areas where its body couldn't go.

Despite having a neck up to 29 ft. (9 m) long, Mamenchisaurus had a very small skull—just 20 in. (50 cm) long.

REARING UP!

Although its long neck possibly meant Mamenchisaurus could already reach up very high, it could probably also rear up on its hind legs to reach food that was even higher up. It may have used its tail as an extra support when standing on two legs.

This reconstruction of the dinosaur's skeleton clearly shows the immense length of Mamenchisaurus's neck.

Like other sauropods, Mamenchisaurus probably had one claw on the inner side of its front feet.

The neck was stiffened with T-shaped bones that helped to support it.

Mamenchisaurus had a small head that held a brain a little bigger than a large egg. An adult human brain, by comparison, is around 20 times the size.

The second part of Mamenchisaurus's name is "constructus," referring to its discovery on a construction site.

SIMILAR, BUT DIFFERENT

All living thing are classified by genus (type) and species. There are several Mamenchisaurus species in the same genus. This means that the different dinos are genetically closely related, but differences evolved between them. The first species described by scientists is usually called the "type" species. Others are compared to this and, depending on how similar or different they are, might be declared a different species in the same genus, a different animal entirely, or a member of the same species.

The Mamenchisaurus neck had 19 vertebrae. They were extremely light and, in places, as thin as an eggshell.

These two animals are from the same genus, Canis, but are different species: one is a wolf (*Canis lupus*, top) and the other a domestic dog (*Canis familiaris*, bottom).

MUNCHIES

An animal as large as a sauropod needed a lot of food to keep it going. Mamenchisaurus might have eaten as much as 1,100 lb. (500 kg) of food a day. Its 80 or so teeth were strong, blunt, and chisel-shaped, and were packed close together. This suggests that the animal bit straight through the vegetation it ate rather than raking leaves from branches.

MICRORAPTOR

Flocks of Microraptor might have soared through the Jurassic skies above China. The bird-like dinosaur is preserved in more than 300 fossils, suggesting it was very common 130 million years ago. It is not known whether they actually flew in groups, as some types of modern birds do, or flew alone.

ASIA

FACT FILE
Name: *Microraptor zhaoianus*
Lived: Hebei Province and Liaoning Province, Inner Mongolia (China); 130-125 million years ago
Size: Weight 3 lb. (1.5 kg); length 16-45 in. (40-115 cm)
Diet: Small animals of many types, fish
Discovered: In 2000 by Xu Xing; named in 2000 by Xu Xing

To scale with adult human

JUST A PHASE

In 1915, naturalist William Beebe suggested birds had evolved through a four-winged phase. Microraptor was not an ancestor of modern birds, though, and has no living descendants.

Microraptor had feathery wings on its arms—as modern birds do—but it also had a long, boned tail edged with feathers.

FLYING ON ALL FOURS

Microraptor had four wings rather than two, which made it unlike most other bird-like dinosaurs. Even so, scientists argue about how well Microraptor could fly, and whether it flapped any of its wings or relied on gliding. Some think it may have climbed trees to launch itself into a glide. Others have pointed out that its body was not well suited to climbing. The feathers on its legs would have stopped it running fast, so it seems likely that it did have some way of moving through the air.

Some studies suggest Microraptor could have powered its flight by flapping, like modern birds, even taking off from the ground.

EATS ANYTHING

Paleontologists have found the remains of different kinds of animals in the gut area of Microraptor fossils. These show that it wasn't a fussy eater: it ate small mammals, birds, and sometimes fish. Some of its teeth were partially serrated and others completely unserrated, perhaps to help it deal with its mixed diet.

TAKING FLIGHT

Some of Microraptor's feathers were proper pennaceous (flight) feathers, 4–8 in. (10–20 cm) long. It had both primary flight feathers (attached to the hand) and secondary flight feathers (attached to the arm), like modern birds.

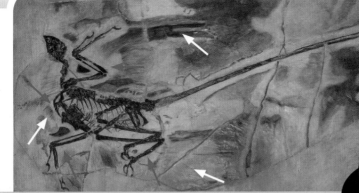

This fossil of Microraptor shows preserved feathers (white arrows) and the white space where they would have been (red arrows).

NIGHT HUNTER

It's possible that Microraptor hunted at night, since it had large eyes. One argument against it being completely nocturnal, though, is that its iridescent feathers would not be visible at night.

Its leg-wings had primary and secondary flight feathers.

SHINY BLACK

All Microraptor's feathers were black and iridescent, so shone with other colors in the light. The iridescence might have made it attractive to a potential mate. Scientists can figure out the color of fossilized feathers with a high-powered microscope, but only if pigment cells, called melanosomes, are present.

Microraptor probably had shiny feathers, like this starling.

MONOLOPHOSAURUS

A large theropod with a strange head crest, lengthy Monolophosaurus roamed the forests of Jurassic China. The dinosaur was originally named after a pub. It was first called Jiangjunmiaosaurus as it was found near an abandoned inn called Jiangjunmiao, which means "temple of the general."

ASIA

FACT FILE
Name: *Monolophosaurus jiangi*
Lived: Xinjian (China); over 163.5 million years ago
Size: Length over 16 ft. (5 m)
Diet: Meat
Discovered: In 1981 by Dong Zhiming (but not dug out until 1984); named in 1992 by Dong Zhiming

To scale with adult human

ONLY YOUNG
Enough remains of the single fossil of Monolophosaurus to tell scientists quite a lot about the dinosaur—except its full size. The skeleton is from a young animal that was not fully grown. All experts can say is that it was at least 16 ft. (5 m) long, the length this animal seems to have been when it died. The end of the tail is missing, so the length has to be calculated rather than measured.

The bones of the head and neck were adapted to be as light as possible, with air spaces and dents.

The lower jaw has 18 teeth on one side and 17 on the other. Different numbers of teeth on each side was usual in large theropods.

Crest

Eye

LIGHT-HEADED
The most noticeable feature about Monolophosaurus is the bony crest that runs from the tip of its snout to just above the eyes. This was made from an extension of the nasal (nose) bone and was hollow. Soon after the dinosaur's discovery, scientists wondered if the crest might have made the sounds the animal made louder. But it's now thought more likely that the air-filled crest helped to make its head lighter. A lighter head would have helped Monolophosaurus to keep its balance.

The bony crest along the nose could have helped the dinosaur to keep its balance.

DEALING IN MYSTERIES

To create a complete fossil for display, experts sometimes have to recreate certain parts. To make decisions about how to do this, scientists examine the parts that they have and try to figure out how this dinosaur resembles others, and which it might be related to. Then they can make informed decisions about how the incomplete dinosaur probably looked. In the case of Monolophosaurus, the rear and front limbs are both missing. To help visitors understand what Monolophosaurus would have looked like, these parts have been recreated in the fossil using plaster.

The fossil of Monolophosaurus on display looks complete, but a lot is based on what experts think the dinosaur looked like.

Monolophosaurus is thought to be a tentanuran, a type of theropod with a particularly stiff tail held out straight behind it.

Like other theropods, Monolophosaurus would have had powerful legs and walked on three toes.

A TOUGH LIFE

The Monolophosaurus fossil shows damage to two of the neural spines of its back caused by injury. There are also marks on the jaw that could be tooth marks from another animal. Paleontologists can learn about dinosaurs' lives from injuries they have suffered and survived. They can maybe match tooth marks to a predator and figure out which dinosaurs ate which others, or whether animals of the same type had ferocious fights. Sometimes they can see evidence of accidents, such as bones broken by a fall, or disease that affects bones and joints.

WORKING WITH ITS HANDS

To recreate the lost arms of Monolosophosaurus, experts looked at other theropods. All theropods had quite short arms, though exactly how short varied among species. Early theropods had three fingers, so it's likely that Monolophosaurus had three fingers, too. The arrangement of their bones and joints meant all theropods held their hands with palms facing inward, so Monolophosaurus would have done the same. Experts could feel confident giving Monolophosaurus short arms with hands that face each other, each with three fingers finishing in long claws.

Paleontologists use fossils to help them understand which dinosaurs might have fought or eaten one another.

PROTOCERATOPS

Sheep-sized Protoceratops survived in a land stalked by predators. Only tough plants grew in the desert-like conditions of Jurassic Mongolia, and these are what it ate. Large numbers of fossils found near to each other suggest that Protoceratops lived or fed in huge herds.

ASIA

FACT FILE
Name: *Protoceratops andrewsi*
Lived: Mongolia; 74 million years ago
Size: Length 6ft. (2 m)
Diet: Tough plants
Discovered: In 1922 by Roy Chapman Andrews; named in 1923 by W. K. Gregory and Walter Granger

To scale with adult human

EARLY FRILLS

Protoceratops was an early ceratopsian, the same kind of dinosaur as the North American Triceratops (pp.43). Protoceratops was probably not the direct ancestor of the North American ceratopsians, but it belonged to the same group as their ancestors. Ceratopsians would have traveled from Asia to North America when the lands were still connected and developed independently there.

Protoceratops had a huge head compared to its body.

Some recreations of Protoceratops give it a tail covered in bristly protofeathers. These were more like a covering of hair than the feathers modern birds have.

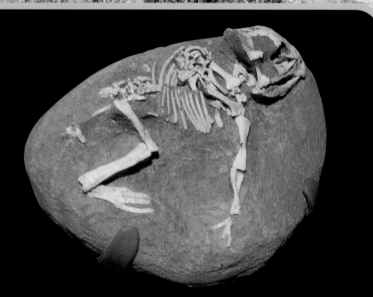

An infant Protoceratops was only around 12 in. (30 cm) long.

BABY STAGES

Protoceratops nests have been found, but with only hatchlings present, not eggs. This suggests Protoceratops cared for its babies for a while. Finding fossils at different stages of development, from embryo to adult, is quite rare.

MISTAKEN IDENTITY

Protoceratops was involved in a case of mistaken identity that led to the small theropod Oviraptor getting its name, which means "egg thief." The Oviraptor fossil was found with a crushed skull, among eggs in what was believed to be a Protoceratops nesting site. Experts thought Oviraptor was stealing Protoceratops's eggs to eat and that Protoceratops stamped on its skull to defend its nest. But the embryos inside the eggs were Oviraptor babies. Maybe the Oviraptor was trodden on by accident.

FIGHTING FOSSILS

An astonishing fossil shows Protoceratops in a fight with Velociraptor. It seems that Velociraptor (pp.158–159) had plunged a large claw into the neck of Protoceratops, and Protoceratops had caught Velociraptor's arm in its beak and broken it. The two might have been killed together by a collapsing sand dune or a landslide burying them alive. Or, Protoceratops bled to death from the wound in its neck, but Velociraptor couldn't free itself from beneath the heavy body.

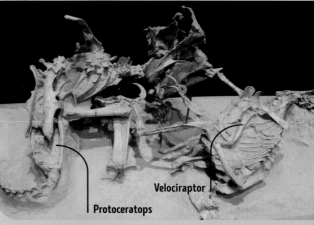

Velociraptor

Protoceratops

Was Velociraptor hoping to kill and eat Protoceratops?

Unlike Triceratops, Protoceratops had a small frill and no elaborate horns. Instead, it had two large bones at the end of its top jaw, which stuck out.

Strong jaw muscles needed to be attached to a large skull. Protoceratops had a huge head, well suited to anchoring these muscles.

The large, tough beak and teeth adapted to grinding, as well as strong jaw muscles, suggest that Protoceratops ate thick plant material.

KEEPING COOL

The fierce midday heat would have made it uncomfortable and even dangerous for Protoceratops to stay out long. Experts think they may have fed in short bursts, sheltering somewhere shady in between.

PSITTACOSAURUS

A stone-eating animal with a parrot-like beak roamed the plains of Jurassic Mongolia. So many fossils of Psittacosaurus survive that it was probably a common sight in its time. Although it had no frills, Psittacosaurus belonged to the group of dinosaurs that would eventually give rise to ceratopsians like Triceratops (pp.43).

ASIA

FACT FILE
Name: *Psittacosaurus mongoliensis*
Lived: Mongolia, northern China; 130-100 million years ago
Size: Weight 44 lb. (20 kg); length 6.5 ft. (2 m)
Diet: Plants
Discovered: In 1922 by an American Natural History Museum expedition to Mongolia; named in 1923 by Henry Fairfield Osborn

To scale with adult human

DOWN IN ONE
The name Psittacosaurus means "parrot lizard." It's named for its beak and skull, which are similar to a modern-day parrot. The sturdy beak suggests that Psittacosaurus ate tough plant matter.

The parrot uses its strong beak to crack hard nuts.

The bristles, up to 6 in. (16 cm) long, might have been used for display or communication. The rest of the body was covered with scales.

At least one species of Psittacosaurus had countershading—it was darker on the top of the body and paler underneath to help camouflage it in the forest.

One fossil of Psittacosaurus has been found with a row of bristles down its back and tail arranged in clusters of three to six.

Gastroliths might have filled a lot of the Psittacosaurus's stomach, as they do in modern ostriches.

CROPPING AND GRINDING
Like many other plant eaters, including some modern animals, Psittacosaurus swallowed small stones that ground down the food inside its stomach. The muscle movements that churned the animal's gut rolled the stones around, tearing up leaves caught between them. When the stones wore smooth, they were no longer of use so would have been vomited up and replacements swallowed.

These stomach stones, called gastroliths, are from the Jurassic period.

STUDYING PSITTACOSAURUS

Many fossils of Psittacosaurus survive. This makes it one of the best-studied dinosaurs. There are fossils representing all ages, from hatchlings just out of the egg and only 5 in. (13 cm) long to mature adults. There are at least eight different species of Psittacosaurus.

This fossil shows a six-year-old Psittacosaurus with a large number of babies.

The front of the jaw formed a beak that Psittacosaurus used to crop plants. Behind the beak, it had sharp cutting teeth, but no teeth for chewing.

INVISIBLE!

Many modern animals use countershading to protect them from predators. Countershading flattens an animal's appearance as it cancels out the shadows cast by its body curves. The "flattened" shape is hard to see against a background the same shade.

The three countershaded ibex are hard to see against the rocks.

The front legs were just over half the length of the back legs. Psittacosaurus walked on its hind legs as an adult, but babies probably walked on all fours.

NOT A TRICERATOPS

Although Psittacosaurus was an early ceratopsian, it did not have direct descendants that resembled later ceratopsians, like Triceratops. We know this because Psittacosaurus had only four fingers, but later ceratopsians had five fingers. Psittacosaurus had cheekbones with little spikes (called jugal horns) that later ceratopsians had, but no other ornaments.

SHANTUNGOSAURUS

An enormous hadrosaur called Shantungosaurus roamed the forests of Cretaceous China. It was the largest of all the hadrosaurs at any time or any place. Not only was Shantungosaurus the largest known hadrosaur, it was also the largest of any dinosaur except the sauropods.

FACT FILE
Name: *Shantungosaurus giganteus*
Lived: Shandung Province (China); 77–70 million years ago
Size: Weight 35,000 lb. (16,000 kg); length 49 ft. (15 m)
Diet: Plants
Discovered: In 1960s; named in 1973 by Hu Chengzhi

To scale with adult human

BIGGER AND BIGGER

It's not clear why Shantungosaurus grew so large. It wasn't the only supersized dinosaur in late Cretaceous China. Gigantoraptor was an enormous oviraptor that lived at the same time. It seems that these animals were getting progressively larger. Perhaps climate change, plentiful food, and pressure from large predators drove them to grow larger. Being larger makes it easier to escape a predator.

Shantungosaurus

Edmontosaurus

Iguanodon

Shantungosaurus was much larger than its relatives Edmontosaurus and Iguanodon.

Shantungosaurus probably needed a long, heavy tail to balance it. Unlike many smaller hadrosaurs, it probably walked on four feet all the time.

Neural spines might have given Shantungosaurus a bobbly ridge along its back.

Shantungosaurus had longer and sturdier front limbs than most hadrosaurs to help support its huge bulk.

THOUSANDS OF TEETH

Animals as large as Shantungosaurus need a lot of energy from food to keep going. It ate only plants, which are less nutritious than meat, so it would have had to eat a great deal. To speed up its digestion, it had around 1,500 teeth to grind food to a pulp before swallowing. They were packed into the back of its mouth, behind its beak. Grinding its food made it easier for the stomach to break it down and release energy for the animal.

Replacement teeth

This tooth battery shows how replacement teeth stack up, ready for use.

BOBBLY BACK

The long neural spines of Shantungosaurus perhaps gave it a bobbly back, with a slightly humped contour. Although they are called spines, in this dinosaur they had blunt, rectangular ends.

Fossil of neural spines from around the hip region of Shantungosaurus.

The head was enormous—the skull was over 5 ft. (1.6 m) long —much larger than T. rex's skull.

Its teeth were arranged in 252 batteries (banks of teeth) with extras stacked ready to use as older teeth wore out. This was possibly the largest number of teeth possessed by any dinosaur.

NOSE NOISE

A large hole near the nose in the skull of Shantungosaurus may have allowed the dinosaur to communicate by calling. Some scientists have suggested that there might have been a bag or flaps of skin, or some other soft tissue, over the hole and that by blowing air into the structure, the dinosaur could make a noise to call to others of its species.

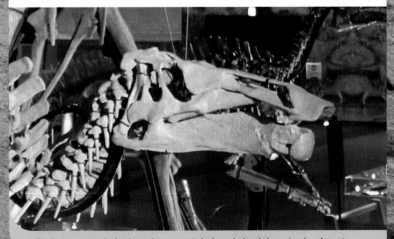

The long, narrow hole along the nose might have helped the animal make noises.

TARBOSAURUS

At the same time as T. rex (pp.46-47) terrorized North America, its close relative Tarbosaurus was menacing Mongolia. Slightly smaller, it lived in the same kind of environment and had the same kind of lifestyle as T. rex. The area where Tarbosaurus lived had woodlands of conifers, rivers, and lots of rainfall.

ASIA

To scale with adult human

NO ONE EATS ME!

Tarbosaurus was the apex (top) predator of Cretaceous Mongolia. Apex predators are important in an ecosystem as they help to control the number of animals further down the food pyramid and keep the ecosystem balanced. If there were no predators, the number of plant-eating animals would increase until there were too many for the plants to support. Then, large numbers of these plant eaters would starve.

Apex predators, like this lion, help keep the numbers of plant eaters under control.

The massive head was balanced by a heavy tail, held out straight behind it.

Tarbosaurus ran on two powerful rear legs.

For a heavy animal walking on two feet, wet, boggy ground carried a risk of sinking. Tarbosaurus's large feet helped to spread its weight.

WHICH CAME FIRST?

Although Tarbosaurus was very similar to T. rex, it lived a long way away from its North American relative. They both evolved to be very similar, or kept similar features from their most recent common ancestor (a type of animal from which they both descended). It's even possible that T. rex evolved from Tarbosaurus (which was an earlier dinosaur).

It's not known whether Tarbosaurus had feathers on any of its body. At least one other Chinese tyrannosaur did, so it is possible that Tarbosaurus was feathery.

Skin impressions from the chest area show that Tarbosaurus had small scales on this part of its body that were just ¼ in. (2.4 mm) across.

Its tiny arms were even smaller than those of T. rex. It's not clear how they were useful to the dinosaur.

TELLTALE MARKS

Fossils can reveal a lot about what an animal ate. Different designs of tooth reveal whether they ate meat or plants. The other fossils found in the same region for the same time show which prey animals were available, but that alone isn't proof that the dinosaur ate them. Bite marks on bones can sometimes be matched to the teeth of a particular predator, too. Bite marks show that Tarbosaurus ate large hadrosaurs and sauropods.

A Tarbosaurus jaw shows it had a powerful bite, useful for holding prey and crunching bones.

BIG FOOT

Fossilized footprints thought to have been left by Tarbosaurus show large feet with scales. One of the better preserved footprints is 24 in. (61 cm) across. Footprints can be fossilized when a dinosaur has trodden in soft mud or sand. This then bakes hard in the sun before filling with sediment, preserving the shape left by the foot.

Footprints can be preserved as dips in the ground.

155

THERIZINOSAURUS

One of the strangest-looking dinosaurs, it took a while for experts to figure out Therizinosaurus. The man who first described the fossil thought it was a huge sea turtle. It took another 25 years for the animal to be correctly identified. In 1970, it was classified as a sauropod and only in 1976 finally recognized as a theropod.

ASIA

FACT FILE
Name: *Therizinosaurus cheloniformis*
Lived: Mongolia; 70 million years ago
Size: Weight 6,600 lb. (3,000 kg); length 33 ft. (10 m)
Diet: Plants
Discovered: In 1948 by a Soviet-Mongolian expedition; named in 1955 by Evgeny Maleev and Anatoly Rozhdestvensky

To scale with adult human

Long, scary-looking claws might have helped to keep Therizinosaurus a bit safer from voracious meat eaters, such as Tarbosaurus. Therizinosaurus was also quite tall, so Tarbosaurus wouldn't have been able to reach its neck easily to kill it.

The tail was probably quite short, as the small head would not have needed much weight at the back to balance it.

THE LONGEST CLAWS

Its massive claws are the most commonly found part of Therizinosaurus. No skull has been found, so we don't have any teeth to judge whether it ate plants or animals. It might have used its claws to haul leaves and branches toward its mouth, or perhaps they were for display to scare enemies, or to attract a mate.

The curved claws of Therizinosaurus were the longest of any animal ever known on Earth!

Therizinosaurus probably had at least some feathers. It might have been fully feathered, or perhaps had just a few scrappy tufts.

At 20 in. (50 cm) long, its claws look as though they would be good for ripping open an animal, but Therizinosaurus was probably a plant eater. Studies of the claw shape and strength suggest it used them to pull branches to reach more food.

Unlike most theropods, Therizinosaurus had four full toes on each foot.

WORKING BACKWARD

Using the bones from other related dinosaurs, experts have figured out that Therizinosaurus probably had a small head, a long neck, a heavy body, walked on two powerful hind legs, and ate plants. More of the skeleton of the related Beipiaosaurus survives, providing useful clues for scientists.

Beipiaosaurus had a small head and a covering of brown feathers, so Therizinosaurus may well have had, too.

VELOCIRAPTOR

One of the most famous dinosaurs from China, Velociraptor was only about the size of a wolf. In 2007, experts discovered that Velociraptor had feathers. These couldn't be used for flight but they would have helped to insulate its body, keeping it warm.

ASIA

FACT FILE
Name: *Velociraptor mongoliensis*
Lived: Outer Mongolia; Inner Mongolia (China); 75-71 million years ago
Size: Weight 33 lb. (15 kg); length 6 ft. (2 m)
Diet: Small animals, insects when young
Discovered: In 1923 by Peter Kaisen; named in 1924 by Henry Fairfield Osborn

To scale with adult human

FEATHERED BUT FLIGHTLESS

When scientists discovered an arm bone with "quill knobs," this confirmed that Velociraptor was feathered. Quill knobs are little bumps on a bird's bones to which feathers attach. Despite the feathers, Velociraptor couldn't fly because its arms were too short and the muscles and bones in its chest weren't right for flying. It might have had ancestors that could fly, though.

Fossils show that the feathers of Velociraptor were deeply attached and not just rooted in the skin-like hair.

Velociraptor's teeth were widely spaced and serrated on the back. This allowed them to lock firmly into the flesh of its prey.

SLASHING OR GRIPPING?

Like many other theropod dinosaurs, Velociraptor had a single extra-long curved claw on each foot. It could have used these claws to hold down a wriggling meal, pinning it through the body as modern birds of prey do. Velociraptor could then bite and tear at its meal with its long, narrow mouth.

Velociraptor could have used the same technique as this bald eagle to hold down small reptiles or mammals.

SMALL PORTIONS

Although there is a fossil of Velociraptor battling Protoceratops (pp.148–149), this was probably quite unusual. Protoceratops would have been too large and heavy for Velociraptor to tackle. Velociraptor probably scavenged large animals when it found them already dead, though. Bite marks on bones suggest it sometimes scavenged Protoceratops. And a bone from a pterosaur with a 10 ft. (3 m) wingspan found in one Velociraptor's stomach is more likely evidence of scavenging than it is of the dinosaur having caught a large pterosaur!

A pterosaur, perhaps like this one, would have been hard for Velociraptor to catch but a lucky find if already dead.

Velociraptor's tail was long and stiff and would have helped it to balance when it was running at speed.

The name Velociraptor means "speedy thief." With powerful leg muscles and long lower legs bones, it could run at up to 25 mph (40 km/h).

SEE AND SMELL

Velociraptor had a very good sense of smell and was probably nocturnal, hunting in the dark. Velociraptor's usual food would have consisted of lizards and other small reptiles, amphibians, mammals, baby or small dinosaurs, and insects.

ZHEJIANGOPTERUS

One of the less showy pterosaurs, Zhejiangopterus had no head crest. It belonged to the same group as the gigantic Quetzalcoatlus (pp.36–37), but was much smaller. The first fossils of Zhejiangopterus were found by a worker in a quarry in China.

ASIA

FACT FILE

Name: *Zhejiangopterus linhaiensis*
Lived: Zhejiang Province (China); 81 million years ago
Size: Weight 17 lb. (8 kg); wingspan 11 ft.(3.5 m)
Diet: Small land animals
Discovered: In 1986 by Xu Chengfa; named in 1994 by Cai Zhengquan and Wei Feng

To scale with adult human

BURIED TREASURES

Quarrying brings many fossils to light around the world by disturbing layers of rock that have built up over millions of years. Quarries often expose rock over a wide area, yielding many fossils of plants and animals that once lived together, telling us about entire prehistoric environments. Removing fossils is a delicate operation that stops work in a quarry and must be carried out by experts.

When an important fossil is found, experts move into the quarry to remove it safely.

The long legs of Zhejiangopterus gave it quite an upright posture when walking. This makes experts think it hunted on land, stalking its prey across the Cretaceous landscape.

SEIZING SNACKS

Zhejiangopterus did not feed or hunt from the air. Its long legs ended in small feet, which would not have been good for standing in mud or shallow water as it would easily sink into soft ground. But its feet would have been good for marching over solid ground to hunt, like a stork. A long beak meant Zhejiangopterus didn't need to extend its head all the way to the ground to snatch up its prey.

A stork can reach the ground with its beak while keeping its head high enough to see any signs of danger.

HIGH FLIERS?

With relatively short wings, Zhejiangopterus was adapted to flying inland rather than over the sea—long wings limit where an animal can fly over land as trees and rocks get in the way. They could probably flap, glide, and ride currents of warm air to soar effortlessly.

MISMATCHED!

Zhejiangopterus looks like it was put together in a hurry! The skull was longer than its rear legs, and both the neck and skull seem stretched, being much thinner than they were long. The neck contained no more bones than the necks of other pterosaurs, but each bone was much longer. To avoid too much weight at the front end making the pterosaur unbalanced, Zhejiangopterus had large holes in the bones of its skull, keeping it light.

Zhejiangopterus had shorter fingers for its size (except for the wing finger) than most other pterosaurs.

Far more than half of the animal's length was taken up by its head and neck.

AUSTRALIA AND ANTARCTICA

There are far fewer dinosaurs known from Australia and Antarctica than from any other continent. That's not surprising for Antarctica. The land is covered by ice and snow so thick that fossils are hidden most of the time even if they lie on top of the rock. In addition, there are very few people to spot any fossils. Although Australia has exposed rock and is inhabited, few fossils have been found there until recently.

Australovenator (pp.166-67)
Australia

Diamantinasaurus (pp.170-71)
Australia

Antarctopelta (pp.164-65)
James Ross Island

AUSTRALIA

Muttaburrasaurus (pp.176-77)
Australia

ANTARCTICA

Kronosaurus (pp.172-73)
Australia

Trinisaura (pp.178-79)
Antarctica

Cryolophosaurus (pp.168-69)
Antarctica

UNDER THE SEA

At the time the dinosaurs were living, Australia was split in two by a sea called the Eromanga Sea, and much of what is now Australia was underwater. Australia has little exposed rock of the right age to hold dinosaur fossils. The rock that is exposed has been subject to harsh conditions for 30 million years, so many fossils have probably been eroded (worn away).

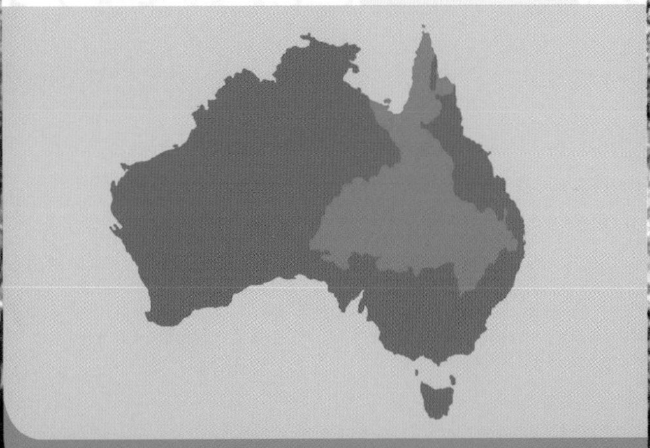

The Eromanga Sea covered much of the land that is now eastern Australia.

FORESTS OF ANTARCTICA

Where there is now icy desert in Antarctica, there were once lush forests and plenty of water in rivers and marshes. Earth was warmer and there were no permanent ice caps at the poles in the Jurassic and Cretaceous. Trees grew at the South Pole, and dinosaurs and creatures like crocodiles lived there. Although only six types of dinosaurs have been found in Antarctica so far, there may be many more from these lost forests, waiting to be discovered far below the ice.

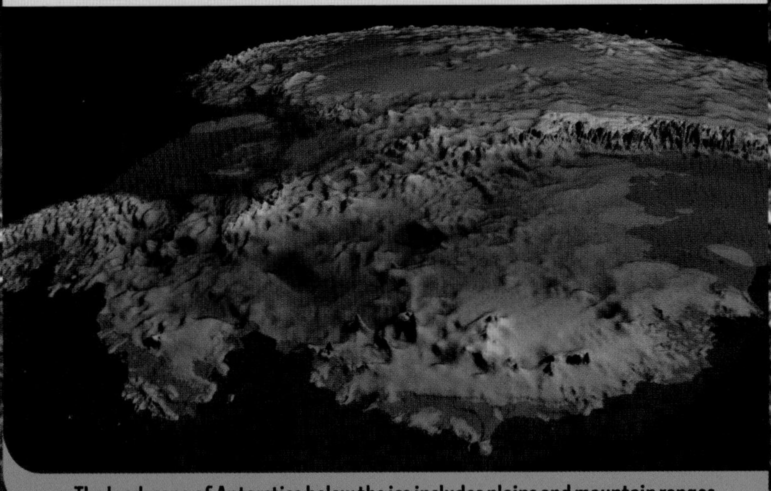

The landscape of Antarctica below the ice includes plains and mountain ranges.

CHANGING LANDS

It might seem strange at first to group the dinosaurs from Australia and Antarctica together. Antarctica is the southernmost land in the world, and includes the South Pole. It's dark for half of the year, and always cold. Beyond the coast, the land is permanently covered with ice hundreds or even thousands of feet thick. No trees or grass grow there. Meanwhile, Australia has many different environments, from tropical rainforest to parched desert. Parts of Australia are some of the hottest places on Earth. Yet these very different lands once lay side by side.

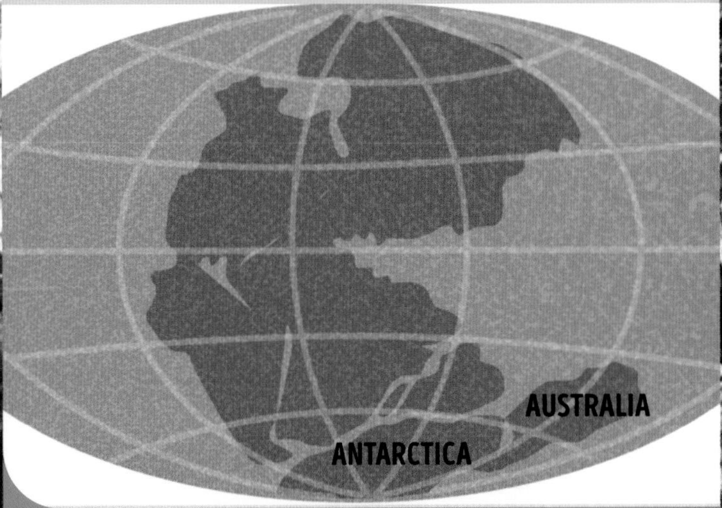

AUSTRALIA

ANTARCTICA

As the supercontinent Pangaea split up, Antarctica and Australia were part of a large southern landmass, as shown here about 200 million years ago. At the end of the Cretaceous, Australia separated and moved northward.

NOT ENOUGH MOUNTAINS

Much of the rock exposed in Australia is of the wrong type and date to contain dinosaur fossils. To find a fossil, deeply buried rock has to come to the surface and be exposed. In places like western North America and Mongolia, land has been lifted as mountains rise up over millions of years, bringing dinosaurs up to where they can be found. There has been no similar mountain-building in Australia. Even if there are dinosaurs under the rock, they are probably a long way down.

STEPPING OUT

There may be few dinosaur body fossils in Western Australia, but there were certainly dinosaurs there. At Broome, on the Kimberly coast, tracks from at least 20 types of dinosaurs are visible at low tide. The largest is 5.5 ft. (1.7 m) long and was left by a huge sauropod. It's the most varied collection of dinosaur footprints in the world.

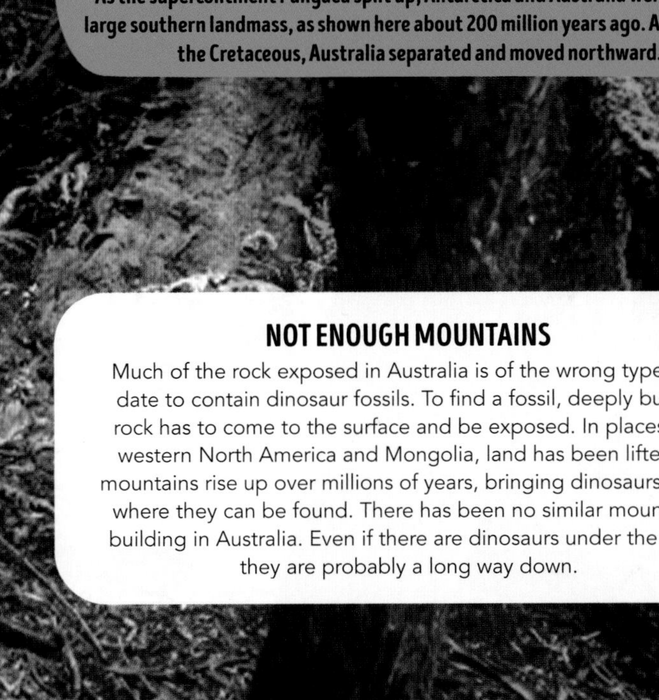

This theropod footprint was made in wet sand 130 million years ago when the area was a floodplain surrounded by forest.

ANTARCTOPELTA

Antarctopelta roamed the forests of Antarctica in the late Cretaceous. It is the only armored dinosaur to have been found on the continent so far. Because of the harsh weather conditions and frozen ground, it took more than 10 years to collect all the parts of the only Antarctopelta fossil.

ANTARCTICA

FACT FILE

Name: *Antarctopelta oliveroi*
Lived: James Ross Island (Antarctica); 74-70 million years ago
Size: Weight 2,200 lb. (1,000 kg); length 13 ft. (4 m)
Diet: Plants
Discovered: In 1986 by Eduardo Olivero and Roberto Scasso; named in 2006 by Leonardo Salgado and Zulma Gasparini

To scale with adult human

IN FROM THE COLD

Antarctopelta was the first dinosaur found in Antarctica, though it wasn't named for another 20 years after its discovery. It was found on James Ross Island, a large island off the coast of the main landmass of Antarctica. James Ross Island is one of only two places in Antarctica where dinosaur remains have been found.

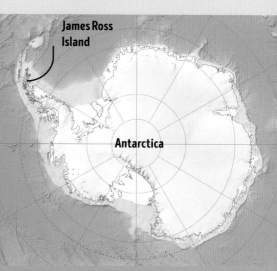

James Ross Island

Antarctica

The ice-covered continent of Antarctica surrounds the South Pole and most of it is inaccessible.

Rectangular osteoderms (bony plates) found with Antarctopelta might have covered its shoulders.

The leaf-shaped teeth of Antarctopelta were similar to those of nodosaurs, but larger. Experts believe they adapted to the type of plants the dinosaur could find to eat in Antarctica, which must have been different from those in North America.

BATTERED BONES

Conditions in Antarctica make it a very difficult place to hunt for fossils and a difficult place for fossils to survive in if they are exposed to the elements. They are repeatedly frozen and thawed, and battered by extremely cold winds. Ice particles in the wind wear away the surface of the bones, so that they easily break apart or even crumble. It was good luck that the bones of Antarctopelta came to the surface when someone was around to spot them and rescue them, though they were already very broken.

Fierce winds and freezing temperatures in Antarctica destroy fragile fossils.

WELL ARMORED

With features of both nodosaurs and ankylosaurs, it's hard to know quite where Antarctopelta stands in relation to other dinosaurs of similar types living elsewhere. Not much of the animal has remained to help scientists. The end of the tail is missing, so we don't know whether it had a heavy, bony tail club like Ankylosaurus (pp.18–19). It was certainly covered in bony plates, or osteoderms, which gave it thick, protective armor against predators.

Today, animals such as the armadillo have protective bony plates.

SPIKE SPOTS

Tiny bony nodules called ossicles were probably scattered over the body of Antarctopelta, between the other osteoderms. The base of a large spike was also found, though it's not clear quite where on the body it belongs. It also had a small spike above each eye.

Large round and small polygonal osteoderms perhaps protected the hips, with ridged, oval osteoderms in a row along the animal's sides.

If the end of Antarctopelta's tail is ever found, that could settle the debate about whether it is an ankylosaur or nodosaur. Only ankylosaurs had a bony club at the end of the tail.

NODOSAUR OR NOT?

Antarctopelta has some of the features of both nodosaurs and ankylosaurs (like Ankylosaurus), heavy, stocky armored dinosaurs, low to the ground. They were covered with bony plates and had a large barrel-shaped belly. But while ankylosaurs had a bony tail club, nodosaurs had an unadorned tail. Ankylosaurs had a broader, shorter head than nodosaurs, and nodosaurs had spines, which ankylosaurs did not.

The front limbs of Antarctopelta haven't survived, but other nodosaurs and ankylosaurs have short, powerful front limbs with five fingers.

AUSTRALOVENATOR

The largest and most complete theropod dinosaur fossil found in Australia is Australovenator. Although around only a third of it survives, many of the most important pieces are there for paleontologists to figure out what it was like, including the hands with claws, a rear leg, and part of the jaw.

AUSTRALIA

FACT FILE

Name: *Australovenator wintonensis*
Lived: Queensland (Australia);
100-95 million years ago
Size: Weight 1,100-2,200 lb. (500-1,000 kg);
length 19 ft. (6 m)
Diet: Small animals
Discovered: In 2006 by Sandra Muir;
named in 2009 by Scott Hocknull

To scale with adult human

A FEW PIECES

Scientists are unsure whether Australovenator should be classed with allosaurs, like Giganotosaurus (pp.62–63), or with the tyrannosaurs, like T. rex (pp.46–47). This might not sound as though it matters, but when we have only a few pieces of a dinosaur, knowing which family it belongs to can help fill in the gaps.

As a theropod, Australovenator would have used its tail for balance, especially when running.

The lightweight, speedy dinosaur has been called the "cheetah of its time."

HANDY HANDS

Australovenator had unusually flexible hands and arms for a theropod. It could move its arms through a wide angle and stretch its fingers further than most theropods that didn't fly. This meant it could grasp its prey and clutch it close to its chest, holding it firm with its long claws while biting it. This was particularly important given Australovenator's relatively weak jaws. Holding its wriggling meal securely could protect its jaws and teeth from being pulled and possibly damaged.

Whether it was a tyrannosaur or an allosaur, Australovenator would have had hands that face each other—"clappy hands"—not downward-facing hands, so it could hold its food.

Australovenator could run fast, which it would have needed to do in order to catch the smaller plant-eating dinosaurs it probably fed on.

FOOTPRINTS

A 3D printed model of Australovenator's foot, reconstructed with its muscle and skin, was used to make footprints in a mix of clay and sand to help understand how dinosaur footprints were made. This also helped to identify some footprints found in nearby Lark Quarry (pp.176–77).

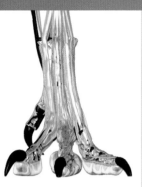

A 3D model of the foot was built up by scanning the fossil.

Despite being a fearsome meat-eating theropod, Austrolovenator's jaws were not as strong, nor its teeth as large, as those of some other, fiercer theropods.

Australoventaor had three fingers on each hand, all with large curved claws that were its main weapon.

SCALES OR FEATHERS

If Australovenator was an allosaur, it probably had scaly skin with no feathers, since the skin impressions that have been found from other allosaurs show only scaly skin. If it was a tyrannosaur, though, it might well have been feathered as many tyrannosaurs were, at least when they were young. If Australovenator was feathery, it probably had feathers like those of a modern ostrich or emu rather than the kinds of feathers that the smaller feathered dinosaurs had.

Like the New Zealand emu, Australovenator may have had long, stringy feathers rather than the types of feathers garden birds have.

CRYOLOPHOSAURUS

The first meat-eating theropod discovered in Antarctica was Cryolophosaurus. Its main feature is a head crest that ran from side to side across its head rather than front to back. However, scientists are still far from certain about many aspects of the dinosaur's appearance.

ANTARCTICA

FACT FILE

Name: *Cryolophosaurus ellioti*
Lived: Antarctica; 195-190 million years ago
Size: Length 19 ft. (6 m)
Diet: Small to medium-sized animals
Discovered: In 1990 by David Elliott; named in 1991 by William Hammer and William Hickerson

To scale with adult human

FEATHERED OR BARE?

No skin impressions of Cryolophosaurus exist, so we can't tell whether it had feathers. Although Antarctica was much warmer when Cryolophosaurus lived there than it is now, there might still have been some snow and ice in winter. The dinosaur might have benefited from insulation. In summer, though, a large animal with feathers might have overheated. Perhaps only young Cryolophosaurus that were less likely to overheat and more likely to get cold had feathers.

This shows Cryolophosaurus with a layer of feathers and a brightly colored head crest, but experts don't know if it had feathers or what its coloring was like.

Cryolophosaurus could possibly have swung its thick, stiffened tail to defend itself if necessary. Perhaps it sometimes swiped at a prey animal, knocking it over.

Cryolophosaurus had sharp, curved claws on its hands.

Glacialisaurus was a prosauropod rather like Massospondylus (pp.114-15), and was around 24 ft. (7.5 m) long.

WHAT'S FOR DINNER?

It's possible that Cryolophosaurus preyed on a prosauropod called Glacialisaurus, which has been found in the same area. This animal was at least as large as Cyrolophosaurus, though. Cyrolophosaurus might have attacked small or sick individuals, or feasted on them if they had already died.

The crest was probably a display feature to make the dinosaur attractive to a possible mate. Individuals might also have judged who was in charge by who had a larger crest.

Tooth marks on some Cryolophosaurus bones suggest the dead animal was scavenged by other Cryolophosaurus.

OWN BONE

Paleontologists often look at other fossils found in the same area to help them decide what a dinosaur might have eaten. There are very few fossils from Antarctica to give us clues. Cryolophosaurus was found with a rib bone in its head and neck area, which was first thought to have come from its last meal. It turned out to be one of its own bones that had moved out of place!

QUITE A CREST

Cryolophosaurus's crest was unusual in that it went across the top of its head rather than along it, and it had ridges that made it seem wavy or corrugated. It was attached at either end to small horns that grew just above the eye sockets. An extension of the bones of the skull, it would have been covered with skin in life. The only fossilized Cryolophosaurus was not yet an adult when it died, so the crest might have grown larger.

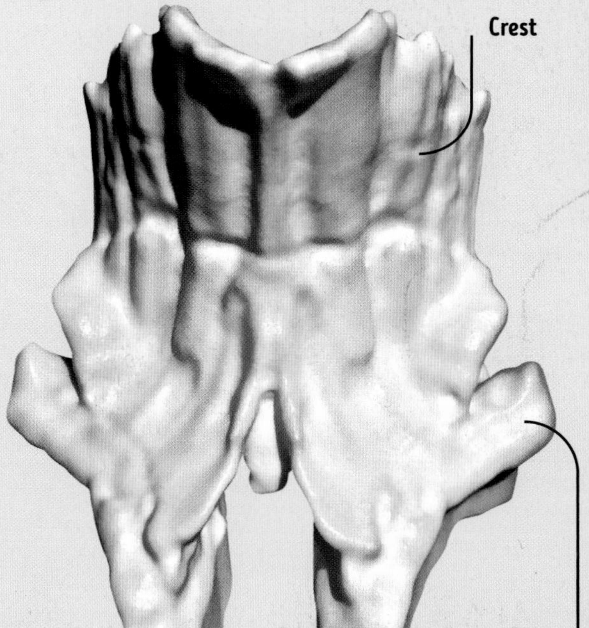

Crest

Horns above eye sockets

A computer-generated model shows the shape of the unusual head crest as it attached to the skull.

DIAMANTINASAURUS

The most complete titanosaur fossil ever found in Australia, Diamantinasaurus is also one of the oldest titanosaurs known anywhere in the world. Diamantinasaurus is thought to be one of the armored titanosaurs, but no bony plates from it have ever been found.

FACT FILE

Name: *Diamantinasaurus matildae*
Lived: Queensland (Australia); 99-94 million years ago
Size: Weight 33,000-44,000 lb. (15,000-20,000 kg); length 52 ft. (16 m)
Diet: Plants
Discovered: In 2005 by Sandra Muir; named in 2009 by Scott Hocknull

To scale with adult human

BONE TANGLE

The fossil of Diamantinasaurus was found in an area that, in the Cretaceous, was threaded with rivers and lakes. The dinosaur's bones were mixed with two others: another sauropod, called Wintonotitan, and the theropod Australovenator (pp.166–67). Experts believe the two sauropods became stuck in mud, probably when going to drink from a river or lake, and their noise and thrashing attracted the attention of a nearby Australovenator. Taking the chance to attack the trapped giants, it then became trapped in the mud and they all died.

Being sucked into the mud was a constant risk for dinosaurs in a boggy area, like this unfortunate Tongtianlong in China.

As a titanosaur, Diamantinasaurus would have had quite narrow hips compared to its shoulders, and a long tail.

MYSTERIOUS MEALS

Diamantinasaurus was a sauropod, so it was certainly a plant eater. Because its jaw and teeth have not survived, scientists can't look to these for evidence of what type of plants the dinosaur ate. In an attempt to discover whether Diamantinasaurus had strong enough leg muscles to support itself on its rear legs while reaching up to nibble treetops, a researcher tried to make a 3D scan of its thigh bone—but the bone was too heavy for the scanner, so we still don't know!

An egg with a dinosaur embryo inside found in Mongolia in 2011 seems to belong to a dinosaur very similar to Diamantinasaurus. The egg is nearly spherical and 3.5 in. (9 cm) across.

Although the head hasn't survived, the dinosaur probably had a small head, large nostrils, and pencil-like teeth.

SINGING DINO

The dinosaur's nickname "Matilda" and the second part of its name refer to a famous Australian song, "Waltzing Matilda." Diamantinasaurus was found in Winton, where the song was written in 1895.

Diamantinasaurus might possibly have had belly ribs, called gastralia—bones that gave extra support to its heavy belly.

NO ARMOR

Most titanosaurs were truly enormous animals—up to 115 ft. (35 m) long and weighing up to 220,458 lb. (100,000 kg). Yet one group of titanosaurs was unusually small: the lithostrotians. The name means "stony skin," and these were the titanosaurs that had patches of bony armor. Diamantinasaurus was small for a titanosaur, so it seems likely that it was a lithostrotian and that its bony plates have become separated and lost at some point over the last 90 million years. Much larger titanosaurs lived in Australia, too. We have no bones, but they have left their footprints and the largest is 5 ft. (1.5 m) across.

The finger bones of Diamantinasaurus were arranged in columns inside the hand.

KRONOSAURUS

The pliosaur Kronosaurus could almost have been designed as a killing machine. Its head, longer than an adult human, took up a quarter of its body and was packed with teeth up to 12 in. (30 cm) long. One of the largest marine reptiles, it lived in the Eromanga Sea, which once divided Australia in two.

FACT FILE
Name: *Kronosaurus queenslandicus*
Lived: Queensland, New South Wales, South Australia; 115–100 million years ago
Size: Weight 24,250 lb. (11,000 kg); length 33 ft. (10 m)
Diet: Large fish, squid, ammonites, plesiosaurs
Discovered: In 1889 by Andrew Crombie; named in 1901 by Heber Longman

To scale with adult human

TOP PREDATOR

The fossilized teeth of a Kronosaurus show wear from biting down on hard objects, and turtle bones found in its stomach area show that it could eat animals with a tough shell. A fossil of a 26 ft. (8 m) long plesiosaur has bite marks probably made by a Kronosaurus. Only the plesiosaur's skull survives, suggesting a Kronosaurus might have ripped the head off and eaten the rest.

Kronosoaurus could eat almost anything, from squid and fish to hard-shelled ammonites (above) and sharks.

Kronosaurus's jaws ran almost the full length of its skull, so it could open its mouth extremely wide. It had twice the bite force of a modern saltwater crocodile.

ROVING THE SEAS

Although most fossils of Kronosaurus have been found in Australia, one has also been discovered in Colombia. A huge sea creature like Kronosaurus could have swam throughout the world's oceans. The areas where its fossils have been found were once shallow inland seas, but that doesn't mean it didn't swim in the ocean. And dead Kronosaurus that sank to the bottom of the deep ocean would never be found.

EVEN BIGGER!

A Kronosaurus fossil found in 1926 was blasted out of the rock with dynamite by a team from Harvard University, who then shipped 8,818 lb. (4,000 kg) of rock to the USA. But it was only when Godfrey Cabot, a wealthy businessman interested in sea serpents, gave $10,000 for the fossil to be cleaned that it was eventually exhibited in 1959, almost 30 years after it had been found.

MAKING A MONSTER

When reconstructing the Kronosaurus fossil, the Harvard team probably added too many extra vertebrae and ribs to make up for missing parts. Around a third of the fossil had been destroyed by erosion and so they used plaster casts of extra bones to fill in the gaps—perhaps too enthusiastically!

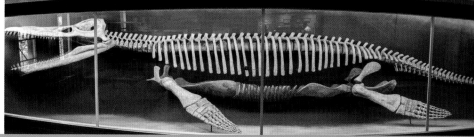

The Kronosaurus reconstruction was at least 7 ft. (2 m) longer than it should have been.

Strong hips meant the animal could push hard against the water with its large rear limbs.

A huge mesh of belly ribs between the front and rear limbs gave extra support and strength to the reptile's body.

Each of Kronosaurus's flippers was 6 ft. (2 m) long.

FLYING UNDERWATER

All four of Kronosaurus's limbs were very strong and used for swimming. The flippers pushed water out of the way by moving up and down, rather like flying but underwater. Kronosaurus reached great speeds by using all four limbs to move itself forward.

Modern sea turtles "fly" underwater using only their front flippers.

LEAELLYNASAURA

A small ornithischian adapted to the long, dark winters of Antarctic Australia, Leaellynasaura scampered through the Cretaceous forests. It could move quickly on its long rear legs, and was small enough to hide under low-growing plants from a predator like Australovenator (pp.166–67).

AUSTRALIA

FACT FILE
Name: *Leaellynasaura amicagraphica*
Lived: Victoria (Australia); 110 million years ago
Size: Weight 17 lb. (8 kg); length 3-10 ft. (1-3 m)
Diet: Ferns, cycads, and other plants
Discovered: In 1989 by Tom Rich and Patricia Vickers-Rich; named in 1989 by Tom Rich and Patricia Vickers-Rich

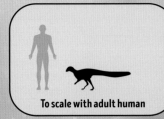

To scale with adult human

A BIT CHILLY

Australia was much closer to the South Pole in Leaellynasaura's time than it is now. The average global temperature was about 50°F (10°C) higher than today, and the South Pole was warm enough for forests to grow. Antarctica was still colder than elsewhere—just not as cold as now! Dinosaur Cove, where Leaellynasaura was found, is on the southeast coast of Australia. At the time Leaellynasaura was alive, Australia was joined to Antarctica, but the land has drifted northward and turned around since then. Leaellynasaura probably had feathers to keep it warm. These might have been fuzzy or even so thick that they looked like fur.

The long tail had lots of small bones, suggesting it was very flexible.

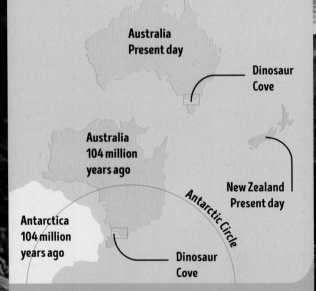

Australia
Present day

Dinosaur Cove

Australia
104 million
years ago

New Zealand
Present day

Antarctic Circle

Antarctica
104 million
years ago

Dinosaur
Cove

A few million years after Leaellynasaura lived, Australia separated from Antarctica. As a result, some Antarctic dinosaurs have become Australian fossils.

EATING AND BEING EATEN

Leaellynasaura ate plants, which grew rapidly in the Antarctic summer, but might have been scarce in the winter when there was little light. Scientists are unsure how dinosaurs dealt with the winter months when plants were in short supply. Some might have migrated north to find food, or perhaps hibernated, sleeping the winter away in a burrow or cave. There is no evidence for either. If Leaellynasaura had large eyes as an adult, it may have stayed active during the dark winter.

GOOD EYES

The darkness of winter, which lasted for five months, might have been more of a problem than the cold. Leaellynasaura had large eyes, as we can tell from the size of the eye holes in the skull. They tell experts that the eyes were large, but not why they were large. It might be because the Leaellynasaura found was not yet adult, and young animals tend to have large eyes for their size.

Animals that have to see in low levels of light, such as this tarsier, generally have large eyes.

With 71 vertebrae in the tail, Leaellynasaura had more than any other dinosaur except some large diplodocoids—but each bone was much smaller than in those animals.

The shape of the inside of Leaellynasaura's skull shows that the part of the brain that dealt with vision was well developed, so we know it could see well.

TAIL TALES

Its tail took up at least two-thirds of Leaellynasaura's length and was probably flexible. Some animals use a flexible tail to hold onto things. Spider monkeys use their tails like a fifth arm to help them swing through trees, for example. Others wrap it around themselves to keep warm as they sleep. This could have been what Leaellynasaura did to protect itself from winter winds. If it lived in a burrow underground, as the related Oryctodromeus did, a feathery tail and a space to sleep away from the weather could have kept it snug and safe.

The snow leopard has a long, thick tail to help it balance when moving about. It also uses it like a scarf to keep warm when sleeping.

MUTTABURRASAURUS

One of the most complete dinosaurs found so far in Australia, Muttaburrasaurus was the first Australian dinosaur to be mounted and displayed. The animals probably lived in large herds, migrating between land that is now in Australia and land that is now in Antarctica.

FACT FILE

Name: *Muttaburrasaurus langdoni*
Lived: Queensland and New South Wales (Australia); 100 million years ago
Size: Length 22 ft. (7 m)
Diet: Ferns, cycads, conifers, club mosses
Discovered: In 1963 by Doug Langdon; named in 1981 by Alan Bartholomai and Edward Dahms

To scale with adult human

WORLDWIDE ORNITHOPODS

Muttaburrasaurus was a type of dinosaur called an ornithopod, similar to Iguanodon in Europe and Ouranosaurus (pp.118–19) in Africa. Like them, it could run on two legs, but probably rested or ambled along on four legs. It was a little smaller than Iguanodon and about the same size as Ouranosaurus. The only distinct difference was a large arched structure over its snout and slightly differently placed and sized nostrils. Similar ornithopods probably lived all over the world, but they went into decline later in the Cretaceous when the duck-billed dinosaurs—hadrosaurs—began to replace them.

The thick, heavy tail was probably used for balance.

MAKING TRACKS

One of the most amazing fossils in Australia doesn't contain a single bone. Instead, over an area of 2,260 sq. ft. (210 sq m) at Lark Quarry, it preserves about 3,300 dinosaur footprints. Most of them were made by 150 small plant-eating dinosaurs, and some were made by a larger ornithopod dinosaur. It was once thought to show a dinosaur stampede resulting from a large number of plant eaters fleeing in terror from a hunting theropod. Experts now believe the trackway at Lark Quarry records the comings and goings of a group of dinosaurs around a water hole. They might have left the footprints over several hours or even days. The "theropod" tracks are now thought to have been made by a large plant eater, such as Muttaburrasaurus.

Muttaburrasaurus is an ornithopod dinosaur, which lived in what is now western Queensland, Hughenden, 112 million years ago.

Muttaburrasaurus had a broad head and a long snout, with a beak at the front and grinding teeth further back for mashing up the leaves it ate.

It probably ate the ferns, cycads, and mosses that grew well in the areas where it lived, but the shape of its teeth suggest it could possibly have eaten meat occasionally.

WHOSE FEET?

To figure out which dinosaurs might have left a set of footprints, paleonotologists look at the kinds of dinosaurs found in an area and what their footprints look like. Dinosaurs of different types make very different footprints. Muttaburrasaurus is a dinosaur of the right type, the right size, and living at the right time to have made the large footprints at Lark Quarry.

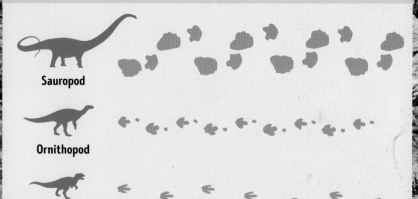

Sauropod

Ornithopod

Theropod

The tracks of a sauropod (top) are very different from those of an ornithopod like Muttaburrasaurus (center) or a theropod (bottom).

TRINISAURA

Only the fourth dinosaur ever discovered in Antarctica, Trinisaura was also the first ornithopod found there. Although Antarctica was warmer than it is now, the cold, dark winters would still have been a challenge for a small dinosaur that relied on finding plants to eat.

ANTARCTICA

FACT FILE

Name: *Trinisaura santamartaensis*
Lived: James Ross Island (Antarctica); 75-71 million years ago
Size: Weight 44 lb. (20 kg); length at least 5 ft. (1.5 m)
Diet: Plants
Discovered: In 2008 by Rodolfo Coria and Juan José Moly; named in 2013 by Rodolfo Coria

To scale with adult human

The fossil of Trinisaura was found out in the open, lying exposed on the ground—it could have been there for many years, as Antarctica is uninhabited.

Experts think Trinisaura had a beak suitable for snipping through plants.

From an animal's skull shape and teeth, paleontologists can figure out how muscles were attached to the jaw, how big the eyes were, and the position of the nostrils.

Trinisaura would have run around on its hind legs, and had a long tail that helped it to balance.

IN GOOD COMPANY

The few pieces of Trinisaura fossil that have been found were in the same area and at the same depth as fossils of the ankylosaur Antarctopelta (pp.164–65) and a sauropod that hasn't been identified. Fossils buried at the same depth in a site are generally from the same time period.

The red layer of these rocks contains fossils laid down over a million years or more—all crammed into rock just 3-10 ft. (1-3 m) thick.

TALKING BONES

Bones of different types have clearly identifiable shapes, so it's easy to spot, say, a rib, a vertebra, or a toe bone. The way these bones differ between animals can reveal a lot. For example, the shape of bones, such as a thigh or shin bone, can tell us whether a dinosaur ran quickly or stomped along slowly.

OUT OF THE WOODS

Scientists figure out what type of landscape a dinosaur lived in by looking at other fossils found in the same place. Fossilized plants show the type of climate at that time, as some plants will only grow in warm, wet places, while others are usually found in cool, dry places. The mix of plant fossils found in Antarctica has enabled scientists to build up a picture of what the forests there might have looked like.

With the types of plants that grew in Antarctica 120 million years ago, it might have looked like this.

Antarctica was ice-free when Trinisaura lived, so the dinosaur might have had scaly skin or feathers.

TOGETHER APART

Just because several types of dinosaur fossils are found together, it doesn't mean that the dinosaurs ran around the landscape on the same days. Layers of rock are laid down over a very long time, and so the other dinosaurs found with Trinisaura could be separated by hundreds, or even thousands, of years. When rock is deposited slowly, animals that lived millions of years apart can be found very close together.

FILLING IN THE GAPS

Even with just a few bones, as there are from Trinisaura, scientists can usually spot similarities that put the dinosaur into a broad group of relatives. Then, by looking at differences within that group, they can narrow down the type of the new dinosaur. Just by looking at the hip, leg, and backbones, paleontologists figured out that Trinisaura was a small ornithopod dinosaur.

GLOSSARY

AMPLIFY To make louder.

ANCESTOR A relation many generations ago; your great-great-grandmother is one of your ancestors.

BADLANDS A dry, rocky place without plants.

BATTERIES (TOOTH) New teeth stacked up below and behind a tooth in use, ready to replace it when it wears away or falls out.

CAMOUFLAGE Coloring and patterns that help an animal to hide by making it blend into the background.

CARRION Dead animals that another animal finds and eats.

COLD-BLOODED Unable to control body temperature; cold-blooded animals rely on the heat of the sun to warm their bodies.

CYCAD Ancient type of plant that has a long, woody stem and tough leaves.

DESCENDANT A living thing that is related to something that lived before; you are a descendant of your grandfather, for instance.

ECOSYSTEM Living things and their environment working together.

EQUATOR An imaginary horizontal line drawn around the middle of the Earth, midway between the North and South Poles.

EVOLVE To change over a period of time to suit the living conditions.

EXCAVATE To carefully dig up.

EXTINCT Died out. When all the animals in a species have died, that species is extinct.

FILAMENTS Thin, threadlike strands, such as hair.

FLIGHT FEATHERS The feathers on a bird's wing that enable it to fly.

FLOODPLAIN A flat area near a river that regularly floods.

HADROSAUR An ornithischian dinosaur with a mouth shaped like a duck's bill.

HEMISPHERE Half of the Earth's globe.

INCUBATE To keep an egg warm, so that the embryo develops and the egg hatches.

INSULATE To keep heat in.

INVERTEBRATE An animal with no backbone.

KERATIN A tough substance that parts of the body, such as hair, scales, and claws, are made from.

LAGOON A shallow area of water separated from a larger, often deeper, region of water by banks or reefs.

LANDMASS A large area of land surrounded by sea, such as a continent.

MICROBE An organism so small it can only be seen with a microscope.

NEURAL SPINE A bony point in an animal's backbone, sometimes forming a spike.

NOCTURNAL Active at night.

ORNITHOPOD A group of ornithischian dinosaurs that could move on two or four feet, and had a horny beak and no armor. They had bird-like feet, usually with three toes.

OVIRAPTOR A dinosaur that moved on two legs, had a toothless jaw, and long arms with claws.

PALEONTOLOGIST A scientific expert who studies and works on fossils.

PREDATOR An animal that hunts other animals.

PREY An animal that is hunted by others as food.

PROSAUROPOD A type of dinosaur that lived before sauropods but in the line that evolved into sauropods.

PYCNOFIBER Hair-like strands that grew from the skin of pterosaurs.

SAUROPODOMORPH A dinosaur with the shape of a sauropod: a long neck and tail, large body, and small head.

SCAVENGE To hunt for dead animals to eat.

SEDIMENT Small particles carried by water, such as sand and mud.

SEDIMENTARY ROCKS Rocks made from layers of sediment that have been compressed by heat and pressure over millions of years.

SERRATIONS The edges of a tooth that are like a saw blade.

TENDON A tough band of tissue that joins a muscle to a bone.

THAGOMIZER The group of bony spikes at the end of a stegosaur's tail.

TITANOSAUR An extremely large type of sauropod.

VERTEBRA One of the individual bones that make up the backbone.

INDEX

PICTURE CREDITS

The publisher would like to thank the following for their kind permission to reproduce their photographs:

(Key: a-above; b-below/bottom; c-center; f-far; l-left; r-right; t-top)

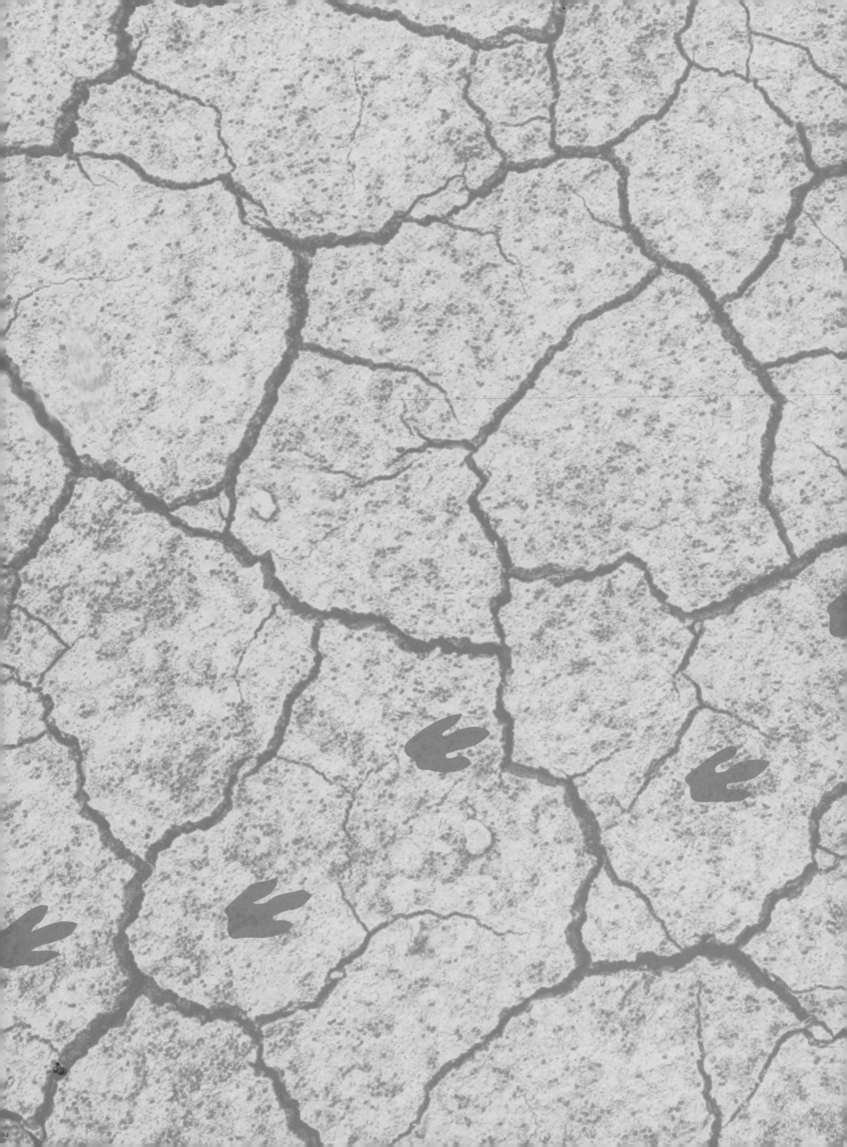